THEOPOLITAN MISSION

THEOPOLIS FUNDAMENTALS
SERIES INTRODUCTION

The Theopolis Institute is a community of pastors, theologians, and students devoted to articulating and disseminating a vision of the church's mission to contemporary culture, a vision that centers on biblical theology and liturgical practice. The church carries on her world-transforming mission by being the church. When the church inhabits the symbolic world of the Bible through the liturgy and communes together at the Lord's table, she becomes a source of light and life to the world.

Theopolis teaches, develops tools, and fosters networks to assist church leaders throughout the world to form thoroughly biblical, liturgical, and catholic churches. The Theopolis Institute is not a church, but is like scaffolding to assist the church in rebuilding God's heavenly city so that it can effectively carry out her mission of transforming the cities of man.

The Theopolis Institute was established in 2013, but its leaders have been working together to formulate and teach a Theopolitan vision of Bible, liturgy, church, and culture for several decades through James B. Jordan's Biblical Horizons.

The Theopolis Fundamentals Series introduces the Biblical Horizons / Theopolis outlook and agenda to a new generation. The early volumes of the series summarize our convictions about biblical interpretation, liturgical theology and practice, and the church's cultural and political mission. The Fundamentals will be followed by a collection of Theopolis Explorations volumes that will examine Scripture, liturgy, and culture in more depth and detail.

For more information about Theopolis, visit our web site at TheopolisInstitute.com.

THEOPOLITAN MISSION

PETER J. LEITHART
PHD, UNIVERSITY OF CAMBRIDGE
PRESIDENT OF THEOPOLIS INSTITUTE

BOOKS
AN IMPRINT OF ATHANASIUS PRESS

Theopolitan Mission
by Peter J. Leithart

Theopolis Books

Copyright © 2021 Theopolis Books
An Imprint of Athanasius Press

Athanasius Press
715 Cypress Street
West Monroe, Louisiana 71291
www.athanasiuspress.org

Cover design: Ryan Harrison
Typesetting: Christopher D. Kou

ISBN: 978-1-7351690-6-4

All rights reserved. No part of this publication may be reproduced, stored in a retrieval system, or transmitted in any form or by any means—electronic, mechanical, photocopy, recording, or any other—except for brief quotations in printed reviews, without the prior permission of the publisher.

Throughout this book, the author has frequently referred to passages from the New American Standard Bible (NASB) published by the Lockman Foundation. Since the NASB passages quoted represent a minimal part of the original document, it constitutes fair use. All other Bible passages were translated by Peter J. Leithart and are reproduced without any further alterations from Hebrew and Greek texts, which are in the public domain.

CONTENTS

Acknowledgements	vii
Blessed City	ix
To the Reader	xi
Chapter 1 Making	001
Chapter 2 Carpenter	021
Chapter 3 Edification	038
Chapter 4 Pilot	058
Chapter 5 Vessels of Salvation	077
Epilogue	097
For Further Reading	102

ACKNOWLEDGEMENTS

Thanks to Jeff Meyers and Alastair Roberts, who both offered their comments on an earlier version of this book. Ashton Moats and John Barach proofread the book and saved me from many errors of spelling, grammar, citation, and detail. Thanks to Chris Kou for typesetting the book, as well as Zach Parker and Jarrod Richey of Athanasius Press for overseeing the publication process.

BLESSED CITY

1. Blessed city, heavenly Salem,
   vision dear of peace and love,
   who of living stones art builded
   in the height of heaven above,
   and with angel hosts encircled,
   as a bride dost earthward move!

2. From celestial realms descending,
   bridal glory round thee shed,
   meet for him whose love espoused thee,
   to thy Lord shalt thou be led;
   all thy streets and all thy bulwarks
   of pure gold are fashioned.

3. Bright thy gates of pearl are shining,
   they are open evermore;
   and by virtue of his merits
   thither faithful souls do soar,
   who for Christ's dear name in this world
   pain and tribulation bore.

4   Many a blow and biting sculpture
      polished well those stones elect,
      in their places now compacted
      by the heavenly Architect,
      who therewith hath willed for ever
      that his palace should be decked.

5   To this temple, where we call thee,
      come, O Lord of Hosts, to-day;
      with thy wonted loving-kindness
      hear thy servants as they pray,
      and thy fullest benediction
      shed within its walls alway.

6   Here vouchsafe to all thy servants
      what they ask of thee to gain,
      what they gain from thee for ever
      with the blessed to retain,
      and hereafter in thy glory
      evermore with thee to reign.

7   Laud and honour to the Father,
      laud and honour to the Son,
      laud and honour to the Spirit,
      ever Three, and ever One,
      consubstantial, co-eternal,
      while unending ages run.

JOHN MASON NEALE

TO THE READER

Theopolitan Mission is a companion to *Theopolitan Liturgy*. They're twin meditations on the relationship between liturgy and culture.

Theopolitan Liturgy explains how the liturgy is the initial Christianization of culture. Existing languages, customs, methods of time-keeping, uses of space, forms of sacrifice, symbols and social habits, gestures and rituals are brought into the liturgy to be transfigured by Word and Spirit. Latin and French and English become liturgical languages, refreshed by the poetry and truth of Scripture. Time is Christianized by church calendars and public space by church architecture. Social relations are transformed by rituals of communion that gather people from every tribe, clan, family, and race at a common table. Liturgy is the first transformation of culture. Liturgical culture *is* Christianized culture.

Theopolitan Mission moves in the opposite direction. In the following pages, I explain how the liturgical life of the church flows out as a rushing, mighty river to wash away sin-corrupted institutions and ways of life. The liturgy is a spring of the Spirit to refresh the world.

This book winds together three threads. The first is an exploration of human "making." We make things because we're made in the image of a God who makes things. We image the Creator in our creativity, and in our creative making we also make ourselves. Since Adam, our making is damaged by sin. Instead of making good things, we mis-make; instead of beautifying creation, we corrupt it as we make sophisticated fig leaves to screen us from the scrutiny of God.

But God is faithful to us and to His creation. He won't let us ruin His world. He sends His Son, the Last Adam, to make a new creation. Jesus' first task is to remake sinners. We're remade as makers by becoming members of His body. The first thing we make is ourselves. By the power of the Spirit, we members of the body build the very body that we are; in Christ, we the Bride build the Bride. Through us, the remade humanity, Jesus fulfills His second task, remaking the creation. By His Spirit and His Word, at His table and among His people, Jesus restores us to right making so we can flow out to remake and glorify creation.

The second thread is about Noah and his ark. Noah is the first godly maker in Scripture. He obeys God's instructions for construction. Because it's made according to God's design, the ark is a vessel of salvation that preserves a micro-world of human beings, animals, birds, and creeping things. It contains the seeds of a new world, which are planted in the new earth after the flood. By building and filling and sailing the ark, Noah ascends to kingship. He's an artist and a craftsman and a gardener, a glorified Adam.

Jesus, the Carpenter of Nazareth, is the new and greater Noah. He builds a living ark from the crooked timber of humanity. By His Spirit, we build ourselves into a saving vessel, where the human race is safe from condemnation. Like Noah's ark, the ark of Jesus contains the treasures of the old world, which are the materials for a new world. As the world is repopulated and renewed by the humans and animals on the ark, so new cultural and political worlds continually emerge from the ark of Jesus' body, His Bride, the temple of His Spirit.

Thirdly, I fill out this meditation on making, mis-making, and right-making by attending to the book of Acts, the great missionary narrative of Scripture. The apostles lead an evangelistic campaign. They announce Jesus as King and establish churches in Jerusalem, Judea, Samaria, and the ends of the earth. Each church is an outpost of the heavenly sanctuary, a temple of the Spirit. By adopting the customs of the apostles—apostolic teaching, the breaking of bread, communion in Spiritual and material goods, continuous prayer—the church challenges and defeats the Satanic powers that rule the world. Because they're courageous witnesses, the apostles take over the Roman ship of state and pilot it through stormy seas, preparing a place where Jesus reigns. In short, the church's mission is the mission of man: to build God's temple in the world, then to remodel the world after the pattern of the sanctuary.

I worry that some parts of *Theopolitan Mission* are too abstract, but my aim is practical. If you're a Christian and a member of the church, the mission of Jesus is *your* mission. You're made to be a maker, remade as a maker when you were baptized into the Last Adam. Your witness, worship, and service build the body of Christ. Through your life and labor, Jesus restores and glorifies creation. It may seem little, but it's not. You've been enlisted into a construction project, than which none can be greater. So follow Solomon's counsel: "Whatever your hand finds to do, do it with all your might" (Eccl 9:10). For, as Paul says, "your labor is not in vain in the Lord" (1 Cor 15:58).

1 MAKING

In the beginning God created the heavens and the earth.
Genesis 1:1

God created man, male and female, in His own image, after His own likeness (Gen 1:26–27). What does that mean?

We get a clue from the following verse: "God said to them, 'Be fruitful and multiply, and fill the earth, and subdue it; and rule over the fish of the sea and over the birds of the heavens and over every living thing that swarms on the earth'" (Gen 1:28). God rules the world He created. Men and women image the Ruler by ruling His world.

We gather more clues in the preceding verses. By the time we get to Genesis 1:26, we know a lot about God. An image of God is *like* God. To figure out what it means to be made in the likeness of God, we should ask, "What is *God* like?"

First and foremost, God "creates" (Heb. *bara'*). That Hebrew verb is used seven times in the first two chapters of Genesis. God creates "the heavens and the earth" (Gen 1:1). He creates great sea monsters (Gen 1:21), and He creates—creates—*creates* man (Gen 1:27). On the Sabbath, God "rested from all the work which God had created and made" (Gen 2:3), and the next section of Genesis describes things generated by heaven and earth "when they were created" (Gen 2:4).

The Creator is a *Maker*. The verb "make" (Heb. *'asah*) is used ten times in Genesis 1, eight times with reference to things God makes—the firmament (Gen 1:7), the lights of the heavens (Gen 1:16), the beasts of the earth and cattle (Gen 1:25), man (Gen 1:26, 31). On the Sabbath, God rests from the "work which He had *made*," that is, "from all His work which He had *made*" (Gen 2:2). In case we don't get the point, the author adds, "He rested from all His work which God had created and *made*" (Gen 2:3).

As Athanasius observed, God's productivity and fruitfulness isn't accidental. He doesn't *become* productive when He creates. It's not as if God were eternally unfruitful and then became fruitful. The Father is eternally productive, eternally generating His Son who is His living Art and His Image. The Son is not created, but He is *produced* by the Breath and Power of the Spirit, the firstfruits of the Father's eternal creativity.

God is a Creator and Maker. If we're made in His likeness, we too are creators and makers. Made in His image, we're made to make.

Man, the Maker

Christians sometimes minimize human creativity. "We don't *make* anything," they say. "We just rearrange what's already there." Maybe you've said it yourself.

Of course, there's a difference between God's making and ours. God says, "Light, please," and there's light where there's never been light before. He says, "Let the waters teem," and *PRESTO!* they teem. He says, "Let us make man," and man is.

We can't do that. We can't create from nothing, simply by speaking. We always use pre-existing raw materials, which we receive as gifts from God. We break them down, mold them, and reassemble them. We don't make animals. We tame them, so they provide work and, eventually, food. We don't make trees. We plant them, cut them down, reshape the wood, and turn it into a shelter. We break and chisel God's stones to make blocks and bricks for temples and palaces. We shear God's sheep, spin their fleece into thread, and weave clothes. Or we wear God's plants—flax, linen, cotton.

God hid some of His most valuable treasures deep in the ground. We mine and smelt His metals to make tools; we dig up gold and polish precious stones to make jewelry. We plant and harvest wheat, grind it to flour, and mix it with other ingredients to make bread. We learn to cultivate grapes, crush them, and slowly ferment them into wine. Eventually, we turn sand into silicon chips and metal into cars and planes and oil into plastics. But we don't *make* wheat, grapes, sand, or oil. We simply transform them.

But we shouldn't over-stress the contrast between God's making and ours. After all, He doesn't make everything *ex nihilo*. *He* makes from pre-existing material too. God makes the formless void, He speaks light into existence, and He appears to make other things by pure *fiat*.

Overall, Genesis 1 shows God shaping and filling the dark, watery earth He creates in Genesis 1:1–2. He spends the first half of the week forming the formless void, giving it light and shape. He spends the second half of the week filling the spaces He forms. But He doesn't fill the world directly. Empowered by the creating Word, the world *fills itself*.

Trees and plants spring up because God speaks to earth: "Let the earth sprout vegetation" (Gen 1:11). Genesis doesn't say, "God said, 'Let there be vegetation,' and *POOF!* there was vegetation." He speaks to *earth*, and *earth* produces grasses with grain and trees with fruit. God speaks to the seas, and the waters teem with living souls (Gen 1:20). The first living souls on earth aren't *directly* created by God's Word. Sea creatures swarm from Word-fertilized waters. Earth brings forth land animals (Gen 1:24). Human beings are the *least ex nihilo* of creatures. Yahweh forms Adam from the *'adamah* (earth), and He builds Eve, the *'ishshah*, from Adam, the *'ish* (Gen 2:7, 21–22).

In fact, once in Genesis 1, something *other than* God "makes." On Day 3, God commands the earth to produce "fruit trees *making* fruit" (Gen 1:11–12). God makes trees, and trees can't bear fruit unless God speaks and gives them the power to do it. But don't miss the punch line: Empowered by the command of God, trees become Godlike. The Maker makes them, and then *trees* make fruit.

By the power of the Creator's Word, earth and sea produce all that is, and the things earth and sea produce continue to fill sea and earth, from God's first Word all the way to today. God doesn't make every single fruit tree or blade of grass that will ever exist during the creation week. He makes trees and grasses with *seed* (Gen 1:11), capable of reproducing themselves. He blesses sea creatures, birds, animals, and human beings with power to multiply, so as to "fill" the seas and the earth (Gen 1:22, 28). Filling is part of the creation process, and the world fills itself.

We can draw this rather astonishing conclusion: Creation participates in its own creation. God completes creation by giving creation power to complete itself. With infinite humility, the infinite God creates by giving *creatures* power to create.

Throughout Scripture, human beings are the most creative creatures, the most inventive makers. Adam and Eve make loin cloths to cover themselves (Gen 3:7). Noah makes an ark (Gen 6:14–22; *'asah* is used seven times). Abraham makes altars (Gen 13:4), and Sarah makes bread when visitors approach her tent (Gen 18:6–8). Yahweh's Spirit equips Bezalel and Oholiab to make the furnishings of the tabernacle (Exod 31:6, 11), and

Solomon makes the temple (1 Kgs 7:51).

Human makings are complex. Cain builds a city and calls it by the name of his firstborn, Enoch (Gen 4:17). No doubt, Cain's city has walls to protect him from avengers (Gen 4:14). It has residents and residences. It has some sort of political order—a town meeting, government by selected rulers, a king. The residents speak the same language, so they can dicker in the market, teach their children, share the day's events of an evening. They adopt common customs of dress, food, work. To live together peaceably, they develop common habits of life and common moral standards. Like most ancient cities, it's likely organized around a civic religion, with a temple and its altar on the central agora.

Cain's descendants produce other new things. Lamech takes two wives, initiating a millennia-long experiment in alternative marriage. Jabal tames livestock, and his brother Jubal is "father of all those who play the lyre and pipe" (Gen 4:20–21). Another son of Lamech, Tubal-cain, invents metallurgy, becoming the first "forger of implements of bronze and iron" (Gen 4:22).

Each of these inventions replicates God's way of making. He lights and forms and fills. *So do we.* We make plans for a house, then frame, roof, and close it in; then we furnish it and, we hope, fill it with joy and life. A dark and unformed patch of the world takes visible shape. We plot out the yard, plow up a garden patch, then fill it with seeds that, we hope, will fill the patch with vegetables. We have a "bright idea" that leads to a business plan. Over time, we fill out the form by finding investors and partners, hiring employees, purchasing equipment, filling an office or a factory. Light, form, fill. Just like God.

To be the image of God is to be a working, making creature. To be the image of God is to be a "cultural" being, always engaged in forging a man-made world within the God-made creation. Enlivened by the Breath of God, commissioned by His Word, we are created to be creative.

I've been saying God uses pre-existing materials to create and make, just as we do. God forms and fills, and so do we. We can see a similarity from the opposite direction too. God makes *new* things. So do we. Of course, we first *receive* God's gifts, but when we've reassembled them, we've made new things, *entirely* new things, entirely new *categories* of things. A table isn't merely a rearrangement of wood. It's a *table*, the sort of human creation that doesn't exist in nature, a created thing God *didn't* create during the six days. When we've learned to spin metals into filaments, and to harness electricity, and to blow glass, we can make a new thing: an electric light.

Think about the humble art of spoon-making, as Nicholas of Cusa invited us to do long ago. There are no spoons in nature, and it's weird to think The Form of Spooniness is secretly hidden within chunks of wood or lumps of metal (along with the Forms of Chairness, Tableness, Coffeetableness). When a man carves a wooden spoon, he's not drawing out a "potential" spoon that's already there in the wood. He's *perfecting* the wood by bringing something entirely new to birth. He gives the wood a new form, so as to make it a new thing. Spoon-making is a Little Bang, a faint reverberation on God's original *fiat*.

We're creative *because* God is creative. More than we realize, we're creative *in the same way* God is creative.

Animals and Artists

I hear an objection: Animals make things too. Beavers make dams. Birds and wasps build nests. Fire ants dig intricate tunnels, the better to attack our bare feet. All these animals create things that didn't come directly from God's hand. Beavers, birds, and wasps give new forms to created things.

Animals make tools too. Apes use twigs to hunt and collect honey, rocks to break nuts, leaves to collect water, sticks to ward off enemies. Chimps strip leaves from twigs to make them suitable for fishing, and other primates have been spotted making moss "sponges" to scrub down their mates. Some fish beat oysters against rocks to open them, and octopi have been known to settle in discarded coconut shells.

Those are impressive achievements and prove that animals share some of the creativity of the Creator. When all is said and done, though, human making is quite different. Think about the difference between human and animal tools. We need food, water, shelter, air, and we make things to help us meet those needs. Tools are conveniences. Strictly speaking, we don't *need* implements to plow, plant, harvest, winnow, and grind. We could dig with our hands, harvest by pulling up plants, grind wheat by stomping on it with heavy boots (but then the boots would be tools!). We *could* twist wool into thread with our fingers and weave the thread without a loom.

Maybe, but we've never done that. We've always been tool-making creatures, not because tools meet our needs directly but because tools make the work of meeting our needs so much more efficient. Tools extend our created powers. I can jump (barely), but if I want to get to Albania, I can't rely on my innate powers of propulsion. I can run (barely), but I can't run to visit my grandkids in Idaho, Washington, or coastal Georgia.

We make tools, but then tools recoil and make *us*. Use a tool for a time, and it stops feeling like an add-on. An experienced carpenter uses his hammer and saw as parts of his body. To a sedentary theologian like me, the keyboard is critical to my thinking process and sometimes feels more critical than my brain. If brain scientists are to be believed (I think they are), my brain changes as I use the keyboard. We're both tool-*making* and tool-*made* creatures. Our makings make us.

Besides, many things we make with tools aren't necessary for survival. Mill stones and ovens are necessary to bake bread, but we don't *need* bread to keep our biological machine sputtering along. We could, like Jesus' disciples, live on what we rub from ears of grain. We don't need the tools of wine-making because we don't need wine. Who needs to go to Albania, Idaho, or Georgia anyway? If we had to run everywhere, my grandkids wouldn't be living in Idaho and Georgia in the first place. My computer is the product of a vast and complex sequence of theories, experiments, designs, and manufacture. But who needs it? Give a real poet a soft clay tablet and a stylus, and he can cuneiform an epic. For that matter, who needs to *write*?

Our making has a uniquely Godlike character. God makes the world He doesn't need. He doesn't dwell in temples made by hands. He isn't served by human hands, as if He needed our help. He gives everything life and breath, for in Him we live and move and exist (Acts 17:24–28). God makes the world out of sheer delight in making, out of a sheer desire to share His life and glory with creatures. Creation is gratuitous all the way down and all the way in. At the inner core, everything God makes is a gift.

No animal makes like *that*. No animal has made even so simple a tool as a screwdriver, and all animal tools have a direct relation to the animal's basic need for food, water, and shelter. Animals don't adorn. Birds build nests for shelter and to store eggs, but there are no schools of ornithological architecture. Beavers don't put solariums on their dams, and no bear decorates his den with wall paintings commemorating his hunting exploits. No animal makes for the sake of making.

That *is* how human beings, made in the image of God, make. Perhaps especially in the modern age, we're surrounded by gratuity, a surfeit of unnecessary comforts and ornaments. Perfumes and potpourri suffuse the air. Colors and shapes catch our eyes. Composers organize tones and harmonies to tickle our ears. We surround ourselves with textured surfaces and mix spices to inflame our tongues. We make playfully, for the sheer delight of making. Our making is erotic, driven by desire for beauty, truth, goodness, and ultimately, by a desire to imitate the God whom we image.

Even when we make useful things, we're not content with mere utility. We don't just make chairs or tables, but well-crafted chairs and tables; not just shelters, but cozy or majestic shelters; not just clothing, but colored clothing with alluring patterns and pictures; not just machines of transport, but flying machines that thrill us and make us feel alive; not just walls and roofs, but painted walls, hung with more paintings, and ceilings; not just communication devices, but communication devices with smooth edges and elegant not-quite-buttons; not just food, but aesthetically pleasing food. For goodness' sake, these days we design *boxes*. Animals play, but no animal can invent cricket or basketball. Animals do wondrous things, but, as Samuel Johnson said, no beast is a cook.

We spend a lot of time and energy maintaining things we make. Once we build a bridge, we need to defend it from use and erosion. Ignored buildings crumble, old tools break, untended gardens are overrun with weeds, paint fades. Our makings aren't once-for-all. But neither are God's. He makes, *and* He providentially cares for the things He makes. He is Creator and Caretaker. Our maintenance work, like our creative work, is Godlike.

Human making verges toward art. Our work aims at glorifying, beautifying, and enhancing creation and human life. Making *per se* isn't unique to the image of God. *God-like* making and gratuitous creativity: *These* are unique to the image of God. To be the image of God is to be an artist. Artifice isn't an add-on to human nature. It *is* our nature.

Art, in turn, makes the artist. That's true in a trivial sense: A painter is someone who paints, a composer someone who composes music, a poet someone who writes poems, a cook is someone who cooks. But art makes the artist in more profound ways. We dwell within our makings, and our cultural creations mold our experience of the world. When the public square is filled with ugly, brutal buildings, we're liable to be anxious, fearful, depressed. When our lived space is full of flowers and trees, we encounter the beauties and joys of creation. When our city is adorned with pillars and spires stretching toward the firmament, our spirits strain for heaven. A dark, formless, empty home will bear different fruit than one that's bright, ordered, and filled with things of beauty.

Man is created as priest to preside at a cosmic liturgy. All our makings are surrounded by praise and thanksgiving. We receive God's created gifts with thanks so that we can re-create them, giving them fresh forms, new uses, enhanced beauty. Then we present the products of our making with thanks and praise. Our making begins in Sabbath and moves toward Sabbath. It's the middle term between first thanks and final thanks, between the rest of the first day and the final rest of the new creation.[1] One day, in union with the Last Adam, we shall deliver up all things to our Father in an eternal act of thanksgiving, an eternal Eucharist.

Empowered by the Word, earth becomes more fully itself by bringing forth plants. Seas become more fully seas by teeming with sea creatures. Trees are fulfilled as trees by producing fruit. *We* are earth and trees, and so our makings, gifted by the Spirit, are also *self*-makings. Made to make, we make ourselves by what we make.

Talking Animal

Anthropologists tell us that human beings begin as natural beings and evolve into culture. That's one source for the euphoria surrounding every small hint that animals use tools. It proves the

---

[1] For more on Sabbath, see *Theopolitan Liturgy* (West Monroe, LA: Athanasius Press, 2019), 83-87.

MAKING

distance between human beings and other creatures isn't as great as we think. Chimps aren't inferior. They're just running a few million years behind and may catch up if human beings stall out.

Scripture tells us the opposite. God breathes life into Adam's nostrils to make him a living soul. He plants the garden, then whisks Adam into it (Gen 2:7-8). A garden is full of natural things, but it doesn't occur unless an intelligent someone organizes natural things into rows and circles and labyrinths. God "plants" the garden (Gen 2:8) with a gate to the east (Gen 3:24).

"Paradise" means a bounded enclosure. Solomon describes his beloved as a "garden locked," a "paradise of pomegranates" (Song 4:13; cf. Eccl 2:5). Jesus promises the Ephesians they will eat the tree of life in "the Paradise of God" (Rev 2:7), a renewed Eden. Adam's first moments are spent watching God organize His park, and then he's placed in that park. Not for a moment is he in a "state of nature." Not for a second is he a purely "natural" being. Culture comes naturally to man.

Before his first day is over, Adam is using language. He doesn't begin with Neanderthal grunts. He doesn't point and gesture. He uses *words*. This is another sign Adam is made in the image of God. God is Speaker as well as Maker. He makes *by* speaking. Ten times, Genesis 1 repeats, "And God said." God speaks light into existence, and a firmament, and a division of waters (Gen 1:3, 6, 9). He calls on the land to produce plants (Gen 1:11) and speaks lights into the heavens (Gen 1:14). He deliberates with Himself before making man, male and female, according to His image and likeness (Gen 1:26-27). Over the course of history, God's crowning work will be to bring man to his full realization as His image and likeness. After He speaks light, He *calls* it light (Gen 1:5). After He examines ("sees") what He makes, He judges it good—not an explicitly verbal act but an act of evaluation. Beginning on Day 5, He blesses creatures of the sea (Gen 1:21), then man (Gen 1:28), then the Sabbath day (Gen 2:3).

The New Testament reveals the fuller truth: God doesn't just speak, but *is* Word (John 1:1–3). The speaking God makes man in His own image and likeness, a speaking creature who can talk back to Him in prayer, praise, conversation, argument. The God who is Word makes human beings by His Word in the image of His Word, so we're equipped to make words and sentences and dramas and epic poems as well as things. I hear that objection again: *Animals* communicate. Birds and monkeys signal with sounds. Scouting bees dance their buzzy dance to pass information to the drones. Your watchdog barks when he sniffs an intruder. But human language is of a different order altogether. No animal talks or writes. Animals can come to know their names. No animal *assigns* names.

Adam uses language to take hold of the world and make it his own. His first act of rule is to name the animals (Gen 2:19). It is a Godlike act of "calling" things by name (cf. Gen 1:5, 8, 10). Adam fulfills the creation pattern in miniature, as observer and participant. God lights, forms, fills, names. So do we. We shape and fill the world and then give names to our creations. In His infinite humility, God receives *our* naming as His own. God names only a handful of things. The rest He leaves to Adam. Whatever Adam calls something, it bears that name, both for Adam *and* for God (Gen 2:19; cf. Gen 2:23 with 3:15). What does God call a laptop? There's no mystery. He calls it a *laptop*. What does God call *me*? He honors my parents by calling me "Peter." What does God call *you*?

By naming, Adam both classifies and discovers, for he learns there is no animal helper suitable to him. It's likely Adam verbalizes created features of animals. There's something "elephanty" about the elephant; the "mammoth" is truly mammoth, and what else would you call a creature so strange as a platypus? At base, though, Adam creates names the same way he creates everything else: He makes them up, *ex nihilo*, as it were. His words don't just mirror the world. God's speech is creative. Adam's names *make* the world into a human world, made meaningful by human speech. Without Adam's names, the world remains un-verbalized, still formless and void.

Have you ever traveled in a foreign country, where all the signs and voices speak an unknown tongue? Disoriented, were you? Think of being plopped into the middle of a completely different world, surrounded by gadgets and gizmos you don't recognize. Are you fearful? Anxious? Giving names makes the world familiar and friendly, a human world submissive to the dominion of Adam and Eve. We inhabit a human world when we inhabit a *named* world.

To repeat my theme yet again: Creatures share in fulfilling creation. The human mission is to co-create creation. The world is meaningful because it's the product of the Word. But we don't merely discover meaning in creation. Meaning is always meaning-*for*-someone. The world has meaning-for-us when we're able to name it. In the image of the divine Word, we *make* creation meaningful.

Human beings are created to be priests who preside at a cosmic Eucharist. We receive the world from God, glorify, name, and fill it with meaning so we can offer it back to God. Our naming is the middle term between first and final thanks. Like our making, our naming begins in worship and is directed toward worship, the alpha and omega of human culture. The world we form by our hands and tongues is fulfilled in the liturgy.

Adam speaks again after Yahweh builds Eve. He names her (Gen 2:23; cf. 3:20), but the initial naming occurs in a burst of ecstatic poetry. With a flourish, he calls the woman "bone from my bones, flesh from my flesh." In the Bible, "bone and flesh" means kinship (cf. 2 Sam 5:1; 19:12–13). Here, finally, Adam says, is a helper who shares my bones and flesh. Though the grammar is different, the phrase resembles superlatives like "holy of holies," which means "most holy place," or "song of songs," which means "best song ever." Adam calls Eve "bone of my bone" and "flesh of my flesh" because he recognizes her as a glorified version of his flesh and bones. Adam glimpses what Paul explicitly declares: The "woman is the glory of man" (1 Cor 11:7).

Adam ends his poem with a play on words, which works as well in English as in Hebrew: She shall be called "woman" (*'ishshah*) because she was taken from "man" (*'ish*). Adam is only a few hours old, and he's already making puns (a sign, perhaps, that humanity is doomed from the outset). Adam speaks as God speaks: freely, gratuitously, not because he *needs* to speak but to say something lovely and good and true. Only human beings do this because only we are made in the image of God. Only we *adorn* our communication with metaphors and similes, with rhymes and rhythms, with music and dance. Animals communicate, but no beast is a poet. Animals make sounds, but there's no animal orchestra.

Before the beginning, God the Father generates His image, the Son (Col 1:15). In the beginning, He makes Adam and Eve as His image. Made in the image of God's image, we're image-makers, symbolic creatures. We grasp the world through linguistic symbols. When it dawns on Helen Keller that the cool liquid she touches is "water," she doesn't just get a name. She gets the *thing*. The Word delivers the world. Linguistic symbols form a *shared* world. When I tell you, "That is water," the substance becomes water for *both* of us.

Symbols make human society possible. We commune with one another by communing together in symbols. We say "we" because we are creatures of symbols. Every society, Augustine says, is knit together by shared signs and sacraments. Because we make and share symbols, we can be more than a pack or a herd. Speaking together, we form one thing, a body. Symbols enable us to share ideas. As symbol-makers, we can con-celebrate the

MAKING

cosmic Eucharist. Sharing common symbols, we mimic the divine society of Father, Son, and Spirit.

Over time, word and thing become inseparable. I don't think of the word "water" as a label pasted on an anonymous liquid. The liquid *is* water, and we experience it as actually, naturally "watery." The symbol contains the thing, and the thing seems to embody the symbol—a mutual indwelling that echoes the mutual indwelling of the Father and His Image, the Speaker and the Word He breathes. We inhabit the world we symbolize as our symbols inhabit us. We make ourselves in making our symbols.

Mis-making

Almost at once, it all goes wrong. Adam speaks the first human words, but the next voice we hear isn't Eve's. It's the serpent's. Instead of using language to praise God and name His creatures, the serpent exploits language's capacity for duplicity and deception. He exaggerates God's prohibition, making God out to be a cheap Creator who won't share good things with His creatures: "Has God said, 'You shall not eat from *any* tree of the garden?'" (Gen 3:1). He contradicts God: "You surely shall *not* die" (Gen 3:4; cf. 2:17). He tells partial truths (Gen 3:5)—Adam's and Eve's eyes *are* opened, and they become as gods (Gen 3:7, 22)—but he uses truth to tempt.

Eve corrects the serpent's initial misrepresentation (Gen 2:2–3), but after she inspects the fruit, she concludes it's "desirable to make one wise" (Gen 3:6). Satan's temptation works. The woman is deceived (1 Tim 2:14). She gives the fruit to Adam, who is with her the whole time, and he eats (Gen 3:6).

Immediately, they begin to mis-make. They see they're naked, vulnerable to God's scrutiny, so they sew fig leaves to "make" aprons (Gen 3:7; Heb. *'asah*). It's the first human artifact, a potent symbol of our distorted, fallen creativity. Instead of re-creating creation as an offering to God, we remake creation to shield us from God's presence. We design and build elaborate cultural, political, social, economic systems to keep God at a distance so He'll leave us to ourselves. We'll do nearly anything to keep ourselves from standing naked before God, anything to save us from that shame. Much of our cultural productions are no more than sophisticated, ingenious, but ultimately useless fig-leaf aprons.

Adam and Eve mis-make because their hearts are damaged. They sin and are alienated from God. They don't make according to God's Word but in response to Satan's lies. Since the fall, our makings express our rebellion. It works in the other direction too. The things we make and the words we speak further entrench us in rebellion. Misshapen works come from deformed workers; misshapen works further deform the shaper. *We* are mis-made by our mis-makings.

When Yahweh arrives in the garden, Adam and Eve talk to Him for the first time. It's not pretty. In answer to Yahweh's question, Adam says he's afraid and hides (Gen 3:9–10), a truthful but tragic response. When Yahweh asks if he ate from the tree, Adam turns accuser and points the finger at Eve (Gen 3:12). Designed as an instrument of praise and dominion, designed to grasp, beautify, and give meaning to creation, language becomes another set of protective fig leaves. The tongue becomes a sword. Adam uses words satanically, to *un*do communion. Instead of joining Adam and Eve in con-celebration, distorted symbols tear them asunder.

Adam comes from earth and works the ground, but Yahweh will make his work more difficult: "Cursed is the ground in relation to you. . . . Both thorns and thistles it shall grow for you. . . . By the sweat of your nose you shall eat bread" (Gen 3:17–19; my translation). Adam will still work in the world, but the world won't cooperate. Alongside grass yielding seed and trees making fruit, earth will bristle with hurtful weeds. Instead of sending down the heavenly rain, the sky will become an iron dome over a bronzed earth (Lev 26:19). Men seek to domesticate animals, but animals kick against the goads. Men build cities only to see them collapse before earthquakes, tsunamis, hurricanes. Men create worlds designed to push God out, but the world is on God's side and rips our flimsy barriers to shreds. We still work toward Sabbath, but now Sabbath becomes a blessed respite from the rat race.

Yahweh's curse isn't just about natural obstacles and disasters. Plants symbolize human beings. Tall, sturdy, fruitful trees portray righteous men (Psa 1:3). Fruitful vines are fruitful women (Psa 128:3). Grains produce chaff, scattered like the wicked (Psa 1:4). Thorns and thistles are dangerous and unproductive human beings, the kind of men who aspire to kingship (Judg 9:7–15), who provide kindling for wildfires (Exod 22:6; cf. Jas 3:5–6), who pierce the heels of the righteous (Isa 27:4; cf. Gen 3:15).

Other people are the primary obstacles to creative making. Lies, slander, and gossip form us into monstrous bodies, a war of organs, all against all. Jezebel pays false witnesses to sway a court against Naboth so Ahab can seize Naboth's vineyard (1 Kgs 21). The wealthy bribe judges to get favorable treatment in disputes over land and rights. Landowners add house to house, squeezing out their neighbors (Isa 5:8–10). Powerful companies lobby and bully to drive small craftsmen out of business. Brutal shepherd-kings devour the flocks they're supposed to guard. Humanity's cultural mission is un-made by social disorder and by political and economic injustice. If our making is going to be remade, *people* need to be remade according to the Word.

Eve is cursed in regard to childbirth ("I will greatly multiply your pain in childbirth") and in her relationship with her husband (Gen 3:16). These strike at the heart of Eve's role in the human mission. Among other things, women are called to join with men to "fill" the earth, but barrenness, miscarriages, and the trauma of labor make that mission more difficult. Eve is created to be a harmonious helper to Adam, but their relationship becomes dissonant. Men follow Adam in failing to guard and then blaming women; women seek to manipulate the men around them.

Grim mis-making continues throughout Scripture. Cain kills his brother and then proceeds, like Romulus, to build a city (Gen 4:1–17). We aren't told anything about life in the city of Cain, but we can surmise it wasn't full of justice and peace. No city founded on the blood of victims can be stable. Cain's descendants show supreme creativity, inventing herding, music, metallurgy, tool-making, as well as politics. But their making is destructive. Jubal doesn't play his lyre and pipe to praise the Creator, Jabal doesn't raise sacrificial animals to offer to Yahweh, and Tubal-cain makes deadly weapons as well as tools to cultivate the earth.

God destroys the world in the flood, but within a few generations after the flood, human beings are right back to mis-making. The men of Babel build a city and a tower to connect heaven and earth. Most of all, they want to make a name (Gen 11:4), which they do, though not the name they hope for (Gen 11:9). That construction project ends when God confuses their language and worship and scatters them over the face of the earth. Babel intensifies the abuses of language that began in Eden.

As speaking and making are perverted, society becomes oppressive and wicked. The major city in Abraham's time is Sodom, a city of sexual perversion, an inhospitable city that welcomes strangers by gang-raping them (Gen 19). In Egypt, Assyria, Aram, Babylon, and Persia, human beings use their Godlike creativity to make cities of death. We devote our human creativity to an inhuman mission of de-creation.

Still today, we devote our ingenuity to making idols. We use linguistic symbols to deceive and sow hatred, to slander and to blame. We fly flags and manipulate national symbols to justify killing and stealing. Human beings invent a magical entity called money, then use it to control, exploit, cover crime, purchase injustice. Our music and art don't enhance the beauty and truth of things but seduce or attempt to convince us of the world's fundamental ugliness. We create under the sign of Abaddon and Apollyon (Rev 9:11). Our mis-made makings unmake the world, and, in unmaking the world, we unmake ourselves.

The Carpenter

We don't know how long Cain or any of his descendants lived. But we know the ages of all of Adam's descendants through Seth (Gen 5:1–32), including Methuselah, the oldest man on record (Gen 5:25–26). We can't construct a chronology from Cain's genealogy, but we can from Seth's. Cain's descendants make all the discoveries, but *time* is on Seth's side.

When the descendants of Seth (the "sons of God") intermarry with the descendants of Cain (the "daughters of men"), things go from bad to worse (Gen 6:1–4). The godly influence of Seth's line wanes, and the world becomes utterly Cainite. Strong men dominate (Gen 6:4). Wickedness becomes great (Gen 6:5). Imagination, so crucial for human creativity, is "only evil continually" (Gen 6:5; KJV). God regrets making man and destroys the world.

The world is saved by a carpenter. Noah is the first rightmaker in human history, a true heir of Adam. He makes according to the Word of Yahweh (Gen 6:13–16): "Noah made (*'asah*); according to all God commanded him, thus he made (*'asah*)" (Gen 6:22; my translation). Instead of making aprons of figs to screen himself from God, he makes an ark of wood in obedience to God. God's Word is the inner essence of Noah's makings. Noah is another Abel, a godly Jabal, who gathers animals and cares for them within the ark (Gen 6:27–21). The ark is a saving vessel, a miniature world, a rescue pod filled with the seeds of a new world. Through this saving vessel, Noah not only escapes the flood but reaches a higher plane of human maturity. He renews humanity's priestly task as he offers the firstfruits of the new creation to Yahweh as an ascension offering. But Noah isn't just Adam redux. He's a new and better Adam, a royal Adam, enjoying Sabbath wine.[2]

Noah the carpenter saves the world, but soon enough, men begin mis-making again. Yet Noah is a sign of hope, a type of another and greater Carpenter (cf. Matt 13:55; Mark 6:3), who makes another saving vessel according to the pattern of the Word—a saving vessel made of people who will serve as a nursery of a renewed creation.

---

[2] For details, see my *Theopolitan Reading*, 65.

2 CARPENTER

Is this not the carpenter's son?
Matthew 13:55

Jesus is the new and greater Noah. He comes at the fullness of time, when storm clouds are ready to burst. A flood is coming (Matt 24:48–49), one that will destroy the ancient world. Roman armies will soon dismantle the temple and burn Jerusalem, and Rome herself will be shaken to her foundations.

The Carpenter of Nazareth (Matt 13:55; Mark 6:3) builds a vessel of salvation to carry the world through the end of the age into a new age. To remake creation, Jesus has to remake *us*. He doesn't build an ark of wood, but harvests from the forest of humanity. He planes, shapes, and assembles a *human* ark. He remakes us as God created the world, as Noah made the ark: He makes according to the Word of His Father.

Jesus makes a saving vessel because He is Himself a saving vessel. His cross is a new ark, sheltering humanity from storm and fire and offering safe passage to a newer world. Joined to the cross, built according to the pattern of the eternal Word, the church becomes the saving ark for all nations and for creation itself.

Scripted Mission

Jesus *is* the Word of His Father, Himself the blueprint of His own construction project. He's the "heavenly man" (1 Cor 15:48–49), the "Word" made flesh (John 1:14). Moses goes to the mountain to see the pattern for the tabernacle (Exod 25:9, 40). Yahweh reveals the temple pattern to David (1 Chr 28:19). Jesus *is* the heavenly pattern, now descended from the mountain into full view of all. He builds a people-ark by impressing the pattern of His own character, His own life, death, and resurrection, on the lives of His disciples. He makes His ark from small-c "christs."

For Jesus and the apostles, Jesus the living Word is the key to and content of the written Word. After His resurrection, Jesus teaches His disciples everything concerning Himself in all the Scriptures. The main story of the Bible, He says, is this: The Christ will suffer and rise from the dead on the third day so that forgiveness and repentance can be preached to the Gentiles (Luke 24:25–27, 44–49). His life, death, and new life are scripted by Scripture. He remakes us by orchestrating our lives to repeat His, by scripting our lives the way His life was scripted. He scripts our lives by Scripture, even as He is scripted.

Jesus accomplishes this through the Spirit. Throughout the Old Testament, the Spirit equips leaders to carry out their mission. The Spirit clothes judges so they can deliver Israel from her enemies (Judg 6:34; 11:29; 14:6, 19). The Spirit rushes on Saul so he can fight and defeat the Ammonites at Jabesh-gilead (1 Sam 10:10; 11:6). The Spirit comes on David to battle the evil spirit that plagues Saul, to fight Goliath, to give him patient hope as he waits for Yahweh to give him the kingdom (1 Sam 16:13–16). The Spirit takes hold of prophets so they can write the Word of the Lord (Ezek 2:2; 3:12–14).

The Spirit does the same in the new covenant. He writes the

law on our hearts (2 Cor 3:3), encourages us (Acts 9:31), intercedes for us as we cry "Abba, Father" (Rom 8:26–28). The Spirit also clothes and equips us for mission. The apostles receive the Spirit of Jesus so they can continue to do what Jesus did. They receive the Spirit so they might become the body of Jesus, Jesus' presence and action in the world. By the same Spirit, the Greater Noah shapes *us* into a new humanity.

From the day of Pentecost on, the Spirit of the risen Jesus is the Spirit of resurrection and new creation. The Spirit rushes on the disciples like a mighty wind (Acts 2:2), like the wind of the Spirit who hovers over formless depth at the beginning (Gen 1:1–2). The Spirit comes like Yahweh entering the garden in the "Spirit of the day" (Gen 3:8; my translation), not to curse but to bless. The Spirit begins remaking His world by remaking the makers who are His image.

Speaking by the breath of the Spirit, the disciples speak other languages. Luke writes a little table of nations (Acts 2:9–11), an echo of the table of nations in Genesis 10. The Spirit performs a miracle of tongues, like the miracle of tongues at Babel (Gen 11). Instead of confusing languages, the Spirit makes it possible for people with different languages to understand one another. Instead of scattering, the Spirit gathers people from all tribes and tongues into one body. Yahweh promises Abraham his seed will bless the Gentiles, and the Spirit of Pentecost is the promised blessing. Since Eden, human beings have misused linguistic symbols. Through the Pentecostal Spirit, language is restored to its original purpose, to facilitate communion rather than to spread chaos and conflict. Pentecost replicates Babel in order to undo Babel.

As Acts unfolds, the Spirit molds the apostles' lives to the scripted life of the heavenly Man. Jesus receives the Spirit at His baptism; the apostles receive the Spirit at Pentecost. Filled with the Spirit, Jesus preaches and performs signs; filled with the

Spirit, the apostles preach and perform wonders in Jerusalem. The scribes, Pharisees, and priests oppose Jesus; the same Jewish elites oppose the apostles. Jesus is arrested and crucified, but rises again. Peter and John are tossed into prison, but are miraculously released to return to their mission, an echo of death-and-resurrection (Acts 5:17–21). By the Spirit, Jesus scripts our lives according to the Scriptures, the Scriptures that reveal Him.

Luke sees the apostolic age as a replay of Joshua's conquest. At the beginning of the book of Joshua, Moses has departed (Josh 1:1–2); at the beginning of Acts, Jesus leaves His disciples. Joshua leads Israel and performs the same signs as Moses (e.g., splitting waters, Josh 3:5–17); Jesus' disciples receive His Spirit and perform the same signs as their Master. Joshua surrounds and destroys the leading city of the land, Jericho (Josh 6); the apostles conquer Jerusalem, Judea, Samaria, and the uttermost parts of the earth. At the battle of Ai, Achan grabs and hides plunder (Josh 7); Ananias and Sapphira lie to the Holy Spirit about their donation (Acts 5:1–16). Joshua is deceived into letting the Gentile Gibeonites join Israel (Josh 9); Gentiles join the Jewish apostles without deception. Joshua conquers the land and then distributes it to Israel as an inheritance. The apostles extend the kingship of Jesus all the way to Rome, claiming the inheritance of Abraham, heir of the world (Rom 4:13).

The Spirit directs the mission of the church by nudging them from place to place. By the Spirit, Peter unmasks the deception of Ananias and Sapphira (Acts 5:3, 9). The Spirit tells Philip to run up to the Ethiopian eunuch's chariot (Acts 8:29), then snatches him away to another place (Acts 8:39). The Spirit doesn't just accompany the apostles, but goes before them, breaking new ground, producing new fruit. When the Spirit falls on the household of Cornelius (Acts 10—11), Peter and other Jews are astonished. They recognize the Spirit has been poured out on Gentiles as well as Jews, and they respond by baptizing Cornelius and his house.

It's a lesson for us too: If we keep in step with the Spirit, we'll find ourselves breathless, rushing to catch up to the Spirit who is always ahead, always surprising.

Wherever the apostles go, they do signs and wonders. Peter and John are wonder-workers (Acts 4:30; 5:12). So are Stephen (Acts 6:8) and Philip (Acts 8:13) and Paul (Acts 14:3; 15:12; 19:11). They aren't just imitating Jesus. Moses was the first to do "signs and wonders" in the land of Egypt (Exod 7:3; 11:9–10; Deut 4:34; 6:22; 7:19), which warned Pharaoh of his approaching doom. The apostles learn from Jesus that the end of the age is coming soon (Matt 24), and their signs and wonders point to that fast-approaching end.

Jesus tells His disciples they will do *greater* things than He did because Jesus goes to the Father and sends the Spirit (John 14:12). Jesus keeps His promise. Filled by the Spirit with the resurrection power of Jesus, they heal the lame (Acts 3:1–8), raise the dead (Acts 9:36–43), give sight (Acts 9:17) and blind (Acts 13:8–11), cast out spirits (Acts 16:16–18). Jesus does all those things, but Jesus never converts three thousand on one day (Acts 2:41–42), never heals the sick with His passing shadow as Peter does (Acts 5:14–16), never heals or expels demons with a handkerchief as Paul does (Acts 19:10–12).

Over and over, early Christian leaders relive the life of Jesus, differently. Stephen performs wonders and bests his opponents in debate (Acts 6:8–10). Mad with jealousy, the elders and scribes stir up the people against him and find false witnesses to accuse him of speaking against Moses and the temple (Acts 6:11–14). After Stephen accuses them of being prophet-killers, they prove him right by stoning him (Acts 7:51–58). Sound familiar? If not, the climax of the story will: As Stephen dies, he echoes the words of Jesus from the cross: "Lord Jesus, receive my spirit," and "Lord, do not hold this sin against them!" (Acts 7:59–60; cf. Luke 23:34, 46).

Peter's final apostolic adventure follows Jesus step-by-step (Acts 12:1–17). Herod seizes Peter and throws him into prison. That night, an angel appears and opens the prison. When Peter arrives at the house where the disciples are praying for him, a woman comes to the door. She reports Peter is free, but no one believes her. Finally, they let Peter in, and he tells them what happened and leaves. Imprisonment, miraculous release, appearance to a woman, report to the disciples, departure: Readers of Luke's gospel have seen it all before. It's a variation on the theme of Jesus' death, resurrection, appearances, and departure to His Father. Jesus the Carpenter makes Peter according to the blueprint of the Word, which is the pattern of Jesus. Like Jesus, Peter is scripted by Scripture.

Paul's life also repeats the life of Jesus. Like Jesus, Paul is a divine warrior, carrying out the new covenant war of utter destruction, eager to cast down every idol. Paul could slip in and out of cities without anyone noticing. He doesn't. When he arrives in a city, he heads straight for the synagogue, knowing that he'll soon be embroiled in battle. In Athens, he debates on Mars Hill (Acts 17:16–34), the most public place in the city, and in other cities he's notorious enough to spark riots. The Spirit of Gideon and Samson emboldens Paul for warfare in public places, in synagogues and town squares. Again, it's a lesson for us: The Spirit drives us into the fray. If you're keeping in step with the Spirit, get ready to fight with the Spirit's weapons. If you're walking in the Spirit, you'll be driven into public places to preach the public truth of the gospel.

As Paul travels through Philippi, Thessalonica, Corinth, and Ephesus (Acts 16—19), he's accused of stirring up trouble, undermining local customs, challenging the authority of Caesar. Gentiles and Jews, Jews and Gentiles: The whole world accuses Paul, as it accuses Jesus.

Acts 16—19 lay out the charges, but Paul doesn't get a

chance to defend himself. Once he gets an opening, he doesn't stop talking. He defends himself to a Jewish mob in Jerusalem (Acts 22), to the Sanhedrin (Acts 23), to two Roman governors—Felix and Festus—(Acts 24—25), and finally to Herod Agrippa (Acts 26). When all's said and done, Paul has been tried by the same courts that tried Jesus—the Sanhedrin, a court of Herod, and the court of the Roman governor. Acts 16—26 form a stretched-out trial scene: first the indictment, then the defense. Paul is another Jesus. Like Jesus, his life is scripted by Scripture, made according to the pattern of the Word.

The Carpenter of Nazareth makes the lives of the apostles like His own. But the apostles also consciously and deliberately live by the blueprint of Scripture. They don't think the fulfillment of the Scriptures ended with Jesus' resurrection. They don't think that God's story wrapped up when Jesus ascended. They decide to fulfill Scripture in their own ministries. They know the drama of Scripture is being played out, with the church in the central role.

The eleven justify the selection of a replacement for Judas by citing Psalms 69 and 109 (Acts 1:20). At Pentecost, Peter tells the crowds that Jesus fulfills David's prophecy about rescue from Sheol (Acts 2:25–28; Psa 16:8–11) and also claims the Spirit's coming fulfills a prophecy from Joel (Acts 2:16–21; Joel 2:28–32). When the Jewish leaders oppose the church, the apostles understand their experience through the lens of Psalm 2 (Acts 4:24–30). At the Council of Jerusalem, James cites Amos 9 as Scriptural support for reception of Gentiles (Acts 15:15–18).

In his defense before Agrippa, Paul describes himself by referring to biblical models. Jesus' appearance on the Damascus Road (Acts 26) is like the vision of Ezekiel (Ezek 1—3). Like Jeremiah, Paul is promised protection from enemies (Acts 26:17; Jer 1:19). Most strikingly of all, Paul describes himself as the servant of Yahweh, who leads Israel in a second exodus. Like the servant, Paul opens the eyes of the blind, shines light into the darkness, delivers slaves from the realm of death and Satan into the light of God (Acts 26:18; Isa 42:6–7; 49:6). Jesus is the Servant. As a servant of the Servant, Paul too carries out the Servant's mission.

It's not just *what* the apostles say and do. It's *how* they say and do it. What Jesus whispered in secret, the apostles proclaim in the public squares. Peter speaks boldly and unreservedly (*meta parresias*) at Pentecost, before an international crowd of thousands (Acts 2:29). In the Spirit, Peter speaks before the Sanhedrin (Acts 4:8) and so passes on the fullness of the Spirit to the other disciples, who speak the Word of God openly, with boldness (Acts 4:31; *meta parresias*). At the close of Acts, Paul is in Rome, but he too preaches "with all openness, without hindrance" (Acts 28:31; *meta pases parresias, akolutos*). It's the last word of Acts and sets the trajectory for the continuing mission of the church. We speak what Jesus spoke. We speak *as* Jesus spoke, with no hedging or holding back, just straightforward truth.

Scripture gives the apostles their boldness in preaching and witness. It gives them their sense of destiny because what they do is as "necessary" as what Jesus did (Luke 24:26, 44; Acts 1:16; 17:3). Paul "must" go to Rome (Acts 19:21; 27:24), just as it was "necessary" for Jesus to die in Jerusalem (Luke 9:22; 13:33). The apostles' confidence in their mission comes from their conviction that what they do is what *Jesus* continues to do (Acts 1:1). They have a sense of destiny because they see their lives as a repetition of the destined life of Jesus.

For Luke and the apostles he writes about, the fulfillment of Moses and the prophets extends to the history of the church. And the fulfillment continues down through the centuries, all the way to you and me. Incorporated into Christ, we're incorporated into His life of suffering and glory as we repeatedly live out Jesus' dying and rising. Our lives, as much as the life of Jesus, are scripted by Scripture, destined to conform to the blueprint.

Still today, the Carpenter of Nazareth is remaking the crooked timber of humanity according to the pattern of the Word.

For many Christians, the Old Testament is a closed book. Today, "typological" interpretation of the Old Testament is seen as quaint, something that childish Christians used to do, until we grew up and learned how to do hard-headed historical research. That's not the apostolic view. As the story of Jesus, the Old Testament is the stuff of their mission. Today's church can do no less. We will not fulfill our mission, which is the mission of the Father through Jesus and His Spirit, unless we follow Jesus' example in our reading and teaching of Scripture. We cannot grow into the ark of salvation unless we recognize Jesus as the One made according to the pattern of the Word, unless we recognize that we are also scripted by Scripture.

Neither Jew nor Greek

Since Adam's sin, men and women have been mis-making the world and themselves. At Babel, rebellious men try to construct a city and tower in defiance of God. Instead of uniting humanity in a grand project, they scatter and divide. In constructing His own saving vessel, His city and tower, the Carpenter of Nazareth makes a single ship from all sorts and conditions of men, all species of human trees.

Unifying the human race is integral to the apostolic gospel. In ages past, Gentiles walked in futility and darkness, excluded from the life of God. They were separated from Christ, excluded from Israel, strangers to the covenant promise, without God and without hope (Eph 2:12; 4:17–19). God doesn't leave them in that condition. Jesus brings near those who are far off. He dies to break down the dividing wall, the wall of Torah that separated Jews and Gentiles (Eph 2:14–15). Jesus' death doesn't just reconcile sinners to God. It reconciles Jews with Gentiles and forms a new, reconciled humanity among Babelic nations. Gentiles are no longer strangers and aliens but fellow citizens with Israel and the holy ones, the saints (Eph 2:14–19).

Acts narrates this apostolic mission of unity. Peter preaches to people of many nations, languages, and cultures at Pentecost. Some are Jews, some proselytes, some Gentile God-fearers (Acts 2:9–11). When Peter is finished, three thousand are baptized (Acts 2:41), and immediately they adopt the customs of the apostles (Acts 2:42–47; 4:32–37).

After persecution breaks out in Jerusalem, many disciples flee (Acts 8:1–2). Philip makes his way to Samaria and begins preaching Jesus as the Christ, the anointed King (Acts 8:4–8). The despised Samaritans rejoice in the good news, receive the Word, and are baptized (Acts 8:5–8, 16). Later, Peter and John go to Samaria to lay hands on the new believers so they too can receive the Spirit (Acts 8:14–17). Like Jerusalem, Samaria experiences Pentecost, and the Samaritans join the Jews of Jerusalem in the one body of the Christ, the one vessel of salvation.

An angel directs Philip south to the road that connects Jerusalem to Gaza, and there he meets an Ethiopian eunuch returning from a feast in Jerusalem, a high official in the court of Queen Candace (Acts 8:25–40). We're not told whether the eunuch is a Jew or a God-fearing Gentile, but he's from a foreign country, an outcast from Israel because of his physical condition (cf. Deut 23:1). He too receives the word and is baptized.

On his way to Damascus to torture, imprison, and kill Christians, Saul encounters Jesus (Acts 9:1–9). Blinded by the bright light, Saul continues on to Damascus, where a believer named Ananias has also received a message from Jesus, telling him to welcome Saul (Acts 9:10–16). Saul's conversion is a turning point in human history, but it won't take unless Ananias is converted too. Like Saul, Ananias needs to see with new eyes. He needs to trust Jesus can turn a violent opponent into an apostle. At the climax, Saul receives the Spirit, his eyes are opened, and he breaks his fast as he's baptized into a table fellowship. At that same moment, the story of Ananias also comes to a climax as he lays hands on Saul and embraces him as "Brother Saul" (9:17). Saul isn't just brought into fellowship with Jesus by the Spirit. He's brought into a new family as a brother to those whom he formerly tried to kill.

Jews, Samaritans, a eunuch from Africa, and a vicious persecutor are joined as brothers. These are the surprising raw materials that become planks in the human ark of the Greater Noah.

Jesus isn't finished. In Caesarea, an angel visits the Roman centurion Cornelius, a God-fearing Gentile, and tells him to seek out Simon Peter at Joppa (Acts 10:1–9). Cornelius quickly sends servants to fulfill the angel's instructions. While they're on their way, Peter sees a vision of a sheet lowered from heaven, full of animals and creeping things of all kinds, and is told to eat them. When he objects, a voice tells him, "What God has cleansed, no more consider profane" (Acts 10:15). When Cornelius's servants arrive, Peter realizes the vision is about them and receives them into Simon's home (Acts 10:23). Formerly separated, Gentiles and Jews share a house for the night.

The next day, Peter and Cornelius's servants go on the return journey, from Joppa to Caesarea, to Cornelius's house, where he's gathered friends and relatives. Peter and Cornelius recount their dreams. As Peter preaches the gospel to the assembled Gentiles, "the Holy Spirit [falls] upon all those who [are] listening." The Jews with Peter are surprised that "the gift of the Holy Spirit [has] been poured out upon the Gentiles also" (Acts 10:44–45). If God accepts Gentiles as well as Jews, Gentiles must be worthy of baptism (Acts 10:47). Through the waters of baptism, Jews and Gentiles are made one. Newly baptized, Cornelius returns Peter's hospitality and allows him and his Jewish friends to stay with him (Acts 10:48).

Soon, the Christians who flee Jerusalem because of persecution end up in Antioch, where they preach the Lord Jesus to Gentiles (Acts 11:20). Antioch becomes the base of the mission to the Gentiles, sending out Paul and Barnabas (Acts 13:1–3), then Paul and Silas (Acts 15:35–41). The Gentile mission isn't just a mission of evangelism. It's a mission of unification. It forms a body of people founded on the truth that God made all men "of one blood" (Acts 17:26; AV). Through preaching and baptism, the Spirit forms a body united by the blood of Jesus.

Bringing Gentiles into the church proves controversial. When Peter returns to Jerusalem after visiting Cornelius, some go on the attack: "You went to uncircumcised men and ate with them" (Acts 11:3). It's true, but Peter explains he is following cues from God, who "gave to them the same gift as He gave to us." God is doing a new thing. How can he stand in God's way (Acts 11:12–18)?

Other Jewish believers, especially Pharisees, demand that the Gentiles be circumcised before they can participate fully in the life of the church (Acts 15:1–5). At the Council of Jerusalem, Peter reminds the elders and apostles that God "made no distinction between us and them, cleansing their hearts by faith" (Acts 15:8–9). Paul and Barnabas testify to the fruitfulness of the mission among Gentiles (Acts 15:12), and then James offers Scriptural proof from Amos 9: God promises to rebuild the fallen tent of David so that all men can seek the Lord (Acts 15:15–18). The Council of Jerusalem imposes essential restrictions on the Gentiles but refuses to trouble them (Acts 15:19–21). Gentiles and Jews worship together in the tent of David, the ark of the Greater Noah.

The new thing isn't that Gentiles are saved. Gentiles have been saved as long as there have been Gentiles. Abraham, the first circumcised Hebrew, meets Melchizedek, priest of the Most High God (Gen 14:17–20). Moses takes his wife from the daughters of Jethro, a Midianite who is a priest of the living God (Exod 2:16–22). When Jews are sown into exile throughout the Mediterranean, they produce an abundant harvest. By the time of Jesus and Paul, there are communities of Jews and God-fearing Gentiles all over the Roman world.

Gentiles being saved is old news. The *new* news is that Gentiles are no longer separate from Jews. In the church, Gentiles are no longer second-class members. Both Jews and Gentiles receive the Spirit. Both Jews and Gentiles are baptized. Jews and Gentiles eat together at a common table and share common prayers. Jews and Gentiles don't become identical. Jews don't give up their ancestral customs, and Gentiles don't have to be circumcised. But Jews and Gentiles become fully equal within the church. Together, they're remade to be makers who fulfill the original human mission. Together, they form the ark where the world will find shelter from the coming storm.

God separates Jews and Gentiles when He calls Abram. Circumcision is the wound in the flesh of humanity, a sign of the separation of Israel from the nations. But God the Creator always separates to reunite. He divides light and darkness in order to harmonize them into the dance of evening and morning. He separates Eve from Adam so the two can become one flesh. He separates Jews and Gentiles so they can be reunited in Jesus. Jesus is circumcised on the cross to heal the wound in humanity, and the church's mission has always been, and must always be, to welcome every tribe, tongue, nation, and people.

In the Spirit, the early Christians pursue unity of mind, purpose, and love (Phil 2:1–2), as we share in a common mission (Phil 1:5). Even before the Spirit falls at Pentecost, the people of the church are of "one mind" (*homothumadon*), devoting themselves to common prayer (Acts 1:14). After the Spirit falls, they continue daily in "one mind" (Acts 2:46). Persecution doesn't divide them, but they respond with common prayer, "in one mind" (Acts 4:24).

Living together with one heart and soul, they sell their property to share the proceeds with those who have need (Acts 4:32). The crowds who hear Philip preach in Samaria come to a united mind (Acts 8:6).

The church even unites her enemies. Because of Jesus, Pilate and Herod become friends (Luke 23:12). In response to Stephen, the Jews of Jerusalem rush at him with one mind (Acts 7:57). In Thessalonica, the Jews unite to bring Paul's hosts before the Roman proconsul, Gallio (Acts 18:12), and the Ephesians are gripped with a single mob-mind when they grab Paul's companions and drag them into the agora (Acts 19:29).

Few features of the church are more crucial to her mission than unity. From the time of Abraham, Yahweh's plan was to reunite the nations under the blessing of God, to undo the fracturing of the nations at Babel. The church *is* and is called to be that united people. Unity is essential to our witness, a witness against divisive principalities and powers, a witness against national arrogance, a witness against ethnic hatreds.

During the age of Christendom, baptism harmonized people from different clans and nations. Teachers from Lombardy, Germany, and Italy gathered at the University of Paris. Spanish monks led monasteries in Scotland and served in the imperial court in Vienna. Regions and peoples of the medieval West retained their local flavor. But each ethnic group locale, with its own customs, was united in the larger whole of Christ's domain.

Over the past century, Christianity has exploded in the southern hemisphere and parts of the far east. As Philip Jenkins has pointed out for years, the statistically average Christian today is a black woman, not a white European male. The church truly is an international people gathered from hundreds of tribes, tongues, and nations, united by a million bonds of prayer, sharing, fellowship, and friendship. With the apostolic history as guide, we can anticipate conflicts over receiving these new peoples.

The issue won't be whether Nigerians and Malaysians and Uzbeks can be saved. As in Acts, the conflict will be over their *equality* in the church. Western Christians have been dominant in the global church for several centuries. That's changing, and we white northern believers need to be prepared to take a subordinate role as deck hands on an ark captained by strangers who have become brothers.

In recent centuries, the churches of Europe and North America haven't had a great track record of unity. Tragically, since the Reformation, the church has fractured. Church splits aren't always bad. Sometimes the church must fracture. Sometimes faithful Christians must separate from false brothers and churches that have become synagogues of Satan. The Reformation was one of those times. Yet for centuries, Catholics and Orthodox, Protestants and Catholics, have refused to seek the kind of one-mind unity that is supposed to characterize the church of Jesus Christ. Our mission is to be a people in communion with Jesus by His Spirit so that we can be a people in communion with one another. God never breaks the church in pieces without intending to join it together again in one Spirit and one flesh. He doesn't dismantle the church except to restore it in a glorified form.

We've grieved the Spirit with our divisions, and we must get back in step with the one Spirit who forms and animates *one* body. We need a massive mission-correction. Jesus is making *one* ark, not a flotilla. Unity is His mission. It must be ours.

Conclusion

As the body of Christ, the church carries on Jesus' mission. Through our work, Jesus saves individual souls, plants churches, and establishes true worship throughout the world. From the beginning, the church does all that. Despite opposition, the Word spreads (Acts 6:7; 13:49). Thousands believe (Acts 2:41; 4:4; 21:20).

Wherever the apostles go, they leave Spirit-filled churches behind (Acts 11:26; 13:1; 14:23; 15:41), each doing what the early Christians in Jerusalem did—devoting themselves to the apostles' teaching, to *koinonia*, to the breaking of bread, to the prayers.

But Jesus' mission is bigger than that. Noah is the first righteous king in Scripture. He builds, commands his family, and rules over birds, animals, and creeping things (Gen 6:13–22). After the flood, he offers an ascension offering, is authorized to carry out capital punishment, plants a vineyard and enjoys wine, the royal drink (Gen 8:20—9:7, 20–21). He pronounces curses against Canaan and blessings to Shem and Japheth (Gen 9:25–27). Noah is an Adam elevated to royalty.

The Carpenter of Nazareth is also a royal figure. He comes in the fullness of time to proclaim the kingdom. Through Jesus and His Spirit, God takes charge of His wayward world. God becomes king when Jesus the Son goes to the cross, rises again by the power of the Spirit, and ascends to take His throne at the right hand of the Father. As Paul says, the gospel heralds the coronation of Jesus the Son of David, declared Son of God with power by His resurrection (Rom 1:1–4). "Son of God" is a royal title in the Bible (2 Sam 7:14; Psa 2:4–7). *This* is the good news: Jesus is king. Not brutal Caesar, not bloodthirsty Herod, not the cunning high priest. *Jesus*, Last Adam and Greater Noah.

If Jesus is king, His body the church is a royal body. Jesus doesn't do anything by or for Himself. We're His body, and His body goes with Him everywhere He goes. We share His sufferings. We receive resurrection life. We're enthroned with Him. Jesus makes His ark-people according to the pattern of His own royal life and so "makes" us a kingdom and priests (Rev 1:6; 5:10). All who follow Jesus are kings and queens. He comes to perfect us, to bring many sons to glory (Heb 2:10). Jesus is exalted as King and will reign until His enemies are placed beneath His feet. He comes to restore and perfect creation so that it becomes all

God intended it to be.

The church's mission is bigger than individual evangelism and church planting. As the body of the Last Adam, the church aims to turn the mis-made world "upside down" (Acts 17:6), which means right-side up. And it does! By making us kings, Jesus renews our hands for making and our tongues for speaking truth. By making us priests, He restores us to our position in a cosmic Eucharist as we receive all with thanks and offer the works of our hands and the words of our mouths in praise. The Greater Noah's first work of making is to remake humanity so we can become makers, fulfilled as the creative creatures we're created to be. Jesus remakes us according to the pattern, the pattern that He is. His mission is to remake the makers so we can resume Adam's original mission of glorifying the world.

3   EDIFICATION

*. . . the whole body, being fitted and held together by
what every joint supplies . . . causes the growth of the body
for the building up of itself in love.*
Ephesians 4:16

God creates by forming and filling. He forms by His Word, and He fills by empowering creation to fill itself. God creates by giving creatures power to create so that, empowered by His Word and Spirit, creation completes itself. This is especially true of human beings, made in the image of the creating and making God. Obeying God's Word and keeping in step with His creative Spirit, we perfect God's glorious world by the things we make and do. In so doing, we perfect ourselves.

Jesus is sent to remake humanity and the world. As the Greater Noah, His first task is to build the ark of the church by choosing and assembling timber from every tribe, tongue, people, and nation. In the ark, He nurtures a new creation. But the principle of creation applies to redemption too: Empowered by Jesus the Word and His living Spirit, human beings complete our own re-creation. By the power of the Carpenter of Nazareth, the living ark *builds itself.*

Does that sound blasphemous? It's not. It's the straightforward teaching of the New Testament. When Jesus ascends, He gives gifts—apostles, prophets, evangelists, pastors, and teachers. Jesus gives gifted men and women "for the equipping of the saints . . . to the building up (*oikodome*) of the body of Christ" (Eph 4:10–13). Who's doing the building—the apostles and prophets and teachers, or the saints? We don't have to decide to get the point. Either way, Jesus equips *human beings* to build His own body.

This isn't a side theme in Paul. When he talks about the church, he talks about the members "edifying" the body; that is, we build the edifice of His body. Paul imagines himself as a craftsman like Bezalel or Oholiab, working to complete God's temple (1 Cor 3:10–17). Even when Paul has to speak severely, he does it to "build" and not to "tear down" (2 Cor 13:10). Prophets speak to build others (1 Cor 14:3, 5, 12), and tongues edify when they're interpreted (1 Cor 14:4). Whenever anyone speaks in the church, it should be for "edification" (Eph 4:29; 1 Thess 5:11). All is lawful, Paul says; but we're called to use our freedom for edification (1 Cor 10:23). We live in love because love "edifies" (1 Cor 8:1). We're called to use the gifts we receive from the Spirit for the common good of the body so the body will be built up into the fullness of itself, which is the fullness of Christ. The principle of ministry in the church is simple: "Let all things be done for edification" (1 Cor 14:26). This is the rule: Do everything you do to complete Christ's body.

We build one another and the body until we attain unity, maturity, the full stature of Christ (Eph 4:13). As we speak the truth in love, we the body grow up into the Head, Christ. Paul's convoluted syntax captures the complex reality: The power to cause the growth of the body comes from Christ the Head. But Christ the Head "causes the growth of the body for the building up of itself (*eis oikodomen heoutou*) in love" (Eph 4:16). As we receive life from the Head, we the body grow *ourselves* into the Head.

The body builds itself. Let that sink in for a moment. Jesus is the Christ, both head and body (1 Cor 12:12). He's what Augustine called the *totus Christus*, the whole Christ. He doesn't perfect His own body—His own whole self—directly. *We're* the hands and tools by which He builds His body. *We* fill up the fullness of Christ. Christ leaves *His own* completion in *our* hands. Jesus is the ark of salvation. As body, the church is the ark of salvation. Jesus makes the ark; in Him, we make the ark that we are.

Change the filter, and we reach the same conclusion. In Eden, Yahweh "builds" (Heb. *banah*) Eve from the rib of Adam (Gen 2:22). She becomes one-flesh, one-body with the first Adam. The Last Adam also has a Bride, born from the water and blood that flow from His crucified body. But God doesn't finish building the Bridal body for His Son. Not even the Last Adam completes the Bride for Himself. *We the Bride* build *ourselves* as the new Eve, Queen to the Last Adam, helper to the Greater Noah.

Tools

We build ourselves as body and Bride because the Carpenter of Nazareth pours out the Spirit of wisdom and craftmanship onto and into us. We build ourselves up as body and Bride through the tools Jesus gives, the tools Jesus energizes by His Spirit. These tools of edification are the "customs" of the church.

As the Word spreads through Jerusalem and Judea, and then out into Gentile territories, everyone recognizes the church as a people with her own customs. They see that Christians want to persuade others to adopt their customs. Jews complain that Christians threaten their customs, derived from Moses and the Prophets (Acts 6:14; 21:21). Some Jewish Christians, especially those who were Pharisees, want the church to conform to the customs of Moses and circumcise Gentile converts (Acts 15:1). Gentiles accuse Christians of teaching customs contrary to the Roman way of life (Acts 16:21).

Jews and Gentiles each have their customs and ways of living. The church appears on the scene as a third race, with customs of her own. Luke tells us early in Acts what these customs are. After the Spirit falls at Pentecost, three thousand new believers join the one hundred and twenty who have been meeting in Jerusalem (Acts 1:15; 2:41). The Spirit gathers them into a separate network of local communities, each following distinctive Christian practices. The Spirit builds the ark through the church's concrete forms of life, habits, ways of speaking, rituals, events, and forms of prayer:

1. Baptism (Acts 2:41).
2. Continuous devotion to apostles' teaching (Acts 2:42a).
3. Continuous devotion to communion (*koinonia*), including communion of goods and property (Acts 2:42b, 44–45).
4. Continuous devotion to the breaking of bread and common meals (Acts 2:42c, 46).
5. Continuous devotion to the prayers (Acts 2:42d).
6. Signs and wonders performed by the apostles (Acts 2:43b).

These customs form the distinctive ethos of the community of Christians. Believers who practice these things experience ongoing joy and gladness (Acts 2:46c) and maintain unity of mind (Acts 2:46a). They're built and build themselves into a unified ark and temple, full of the joy of festivity.

These don't look like the kind of tools we need to make a new humanity as an ark for the world. They don't look like customs that will overturn the world, transform the mis-makings of human culture, and move the devastated world toward justice and peace. But if we despise these customs, we're seeing with eyes of flesh.

For these are Spiritual weapons and tools, designed to turn the world upside down (Acts 17:6).

Baptism into the Name

Peter compares the flood to baptism (1 Pet 3:18–22) because baptism, like the flood, rescues the early Christians from their perverse generation (Acts 2:40). Jesus condemns the "adulterous generation" during His own ministry (Matt 12:39, 41–45; 16:4; 17:17) and warns that a flood-like judgment looms over "this generation" (Matt 23:36; 24:34, 37–38; Luke 17:26–27; cf. Matt 7:26–27; Luke 6:47–49). God is preparing one final deluge to wash away the ancient order of Israel-and-empire. When it comes, those who cling to the true Bridegroom, Jesus, will be saved.

Baptism assembles the material and crew for Jesus' ark. As we've seen, each new group is incorporated into the church by baptism. Philip baptizes Samaritans (Acts 8:12–13), then the Spirit sweeps him away to meet an Ethiopian eunuch, whom he baptizes at an oasis in the desert (Acts 8:36–38). When the Spirit falls on the household of the Gentile God-fearer, Cornelius, Peter determines they should be baptized (Acts 10:48). At Philippi, Paul and Silas baptize the jailer and his household (Acts 16:33), and many in Corinth are baptized (Acts 18:8). Through baptism, Jesus makes His one people. As the church baptizes, she makes herself the one new man.

Noah's ark is a sacred space. Like other sanctuaries in the Bible, it's measured and constructed according to a revealed blueprint (Gen 6:15; Exod 25:9, 40). It has three decks (Gen 6:16), as the tabernacle and temple have three zones: the court, the Holy Place, and the Most Holy Place. Like later sanctuaries, it's filled with animals (Gen 6:19–20). During the flood, the ark ascends closer and closer to the firmament, above the highest mountains. It becomes a link between heaven and earth, the very gate of God. After the flood, it comes to rest on an Eden-like mountain (Gen 8:4), and Noah offers clean animals as ascension offerings on an altar built in front of the ark (Gen 8:20–21). Noah's ark is a floating ziggurat, a nautical holy mountain.[1]

The ark of the Carpenter of Nazareth is likewise a holy place, a temple of the Spirit. The baptized are living stones and planks in God's house, prepared to offer Spiritual sacrifices of praise (1 Pet 2:5). The baptized are safe in the sanctuary of the ark. The baptized are also called to serve as priests in the Spirit's ark-temple.

In the church, priestly service means practicing Christian customs—the apostles' teaching, the breaking of bread, the prayers. By the Spirit, baptism equips us to be wise craftsmen in building His church. In baptism, the Carpenter of Nazareth fills our hands with tools to edify His body. Luke uses verb forms that emphasize the "continuous" nature of these customs. They are "*continually* devoted" to the practices of the church. Luke alludes to the Hebrew word *tamid*, which describes the "continuous" liturgical practices carried out in the temple in Jerusalem (Exod 27:20; 28:29–30, 42; Lev 6:13; 24:2). Priests in the old order continually carry out the liturgy of temple worship. The baptized are priests of the new temple and continually carry out the liturgy of life that makes up the life of the church. Baptism restores us to our priestly calling so that our making is embedded in a cycle of thanks and praise.

Cleansed and sanctified to labor in the holy house of the Spirit, the baptized are also enlisted to carry out public service in the world. We present our clean bodies as living and holy sacrifices, performing the good and acceptable liturgy of common life (Rom 12:1–2). We devote the members of our body to the

---

[1] For more on biblical sanctuaries, see *Theopolitan Liturgy* (Monroe, LA: Athanasius Press, 2019), ch. 1.

justice of God's kingdom (Rom 6:1–14). The baptized follow Jesus by practicing hospitality, blessing persecutors, refusing vengeance, overcoming evil with good (Rom 12:13–14, 19–21).

The church fathers describe baptism as a "seal" and often compare it to the brand on an animal, the owner's mark on a slave, or the regimental tattoo on a Roman soldier. Baptized into the name of Jesus, disciples of Jesus wear His name. We're called not only to maintain the Lord's house, the church, but to battle giants in the land, taking down principalities and powers and everything that stands against Jesus.

Pattern of Teaching

Jesus teaches His disciples "everything concerning Himself in all the Scriptures." The apostles learn the lesson well. Whenever they teach, they teach from the Scriptures, showing that Jesus is the message of Moses and the prophets.

At Pentecost, Peter quotes a section of Psalm 16 and concludes that Jesus, not David, is the One saved from Sheol (Acts 2:25–29). In the next breath, he cites Psalm 132, a promise that David's Seed will sit on his throne. He applies it to Jesus (Acts 2:30). Preaching at the portico of Solomon after healing a lame man, Peter quotes Deuteronomy 18 to show that Jesus is the new Moses-like Prophet (Acts 3:22).

According to Peter, Jesus is the "stone which was rejected" (Acts 4:11; Psa 118:22), and Philip teaches the Ethiopian eunuch that Jesus is the suffering Servant of Isaiah 53 (Acts 8:26–35). Paul says Psalm 2's declaration about Yahweh's Son is fulfilled in the resurrection of Jesus (Acts 13:32–33). At Thessalonica, Paul teaches from the Scriptures that "the Christ had to suffer and rise again from the dead," a virtual quotation from Jesus' own teaching (Acts 17:2–3). Later, Paul assures Herod Agrippa he believes Moses and the prophets, who teach "that the Christ was to suffer

EDIFICATION

and that by reason of resurrection from the dead He should be the first to proclaim light both to the people and to the Gentiles" (Acts 26:22–23).

The apostles don't cherry-pick quotations from the Old Testament. They retell the story of the Old Testament as a story that climaxes in Jesus. When Peter and John are brought before the Sanhedrin, they remind the Jewish leaders of God's promise to Abraham: "in your seed all the families of the earth shall be blessed" (Acts 3:25; Gen 22:18). The God of Abraham, Isaac, and Jacob sends Jesus to fulfill this promise and has "glorified His servant Jesus" by raising Him from the dead and by elevating Him to heaven (Acts 3:13–21).

Stephen preaches about Abraham's call to leave his country for the land of promise (Acts 7:2–8), tells the life of Joseph (Acts 7:9–16), and recounts the exodus, focusing on Moses' two visitations to deliver Israel (Acts 7:17–41). Instead of listening to Moses, Israel rejects him and goes after other gods, both in the wilderness and in the land (Acts 7:42–43). Stephen charges his hearers with repeating the sin of their fathers. Israel has always persecuted prophets and killed those sent to them (Acts 7:51–52). They rejected Jesus just as they rejected Moses. Now they reject Stephen himself.

At Pisidian Antioch, Paul reminds the Jews they're chosen and redeemed from Egypt to receive the inheritance of the land (Acts 13:16–19). After Saul, Yahweh raises up David and promises David's seed will sit on His throne forever (Acts 13:21–22). Jesus is the fulfillment of this promise, but the Jews put Him to death. But God raises and enthrones Him (Acts 13:30–33), so the promise made to the fathers can be fulfilled, forgiveness can be preached, and Jews can be freed from everything the law was powerless to achieve (Acts 13:32, 38–39). Paul's sermon is about Israel's story, which culminates in the sufferings and glory of Jesus the Christ.

Paul preaches to Gentile audiences too, and the emphasis is different. He tells Gentiles about the God who creates all things, shows Himself even to ignorant Gentiles, and now holds all men to account (Acts 14:15-17; 17:16-31). These sermons also hinge on the coming of Jesus. Because of Jesus, God no longer allows nations to go their own way (Acts 14:16). Because of Jesus, the times of ignorance have come to an end, and God is calling all men to repent. Athenians aren't permitted to worship the "unknown god" anymore, since Paul has made Him known. For the Gentile world, the sign of the new age is the appointment of Jesus, the *resurrected* Jesus, as Judge of the world (Acts 17:30-31). According to Paul, Jesus is King and Judge of Gentiles as well as Jews. Jesus isn't just the center of Israel's history. He's the center of human history.

By the Spirit, this pattern of teaching—which is the pattern of Jesus' own life—is imprinted on the church. Through such teaching, the church builds herself up as body, Bride, and ark because through such teaching, the church is conformed to the pattern from heaven. When the church strays, the Spirit speaks in Scripture to call her back to Jesus. Through apostolic teaching, we the members of the church learn how to build, to follow the Carpenter of Nazareth in making rightly. Apostolic teaching unveils the pattern of Christ, which is the blueprint for our lives, for the church, for the world.

Communion in the Spirit

Baptized into the Spirit-filled body of disciples, the converts on Pentecost begin to live a Pentecostal body life. Luke sums it up in one word: *koinonia*, "fellowship" (Acts 2:42). For many Christians, "fellowship" involves potlucks and post-worship conversations about football or politics. Luke has something thicker and more challenging in mind. For ancient Greeks, *koinonia* is a political term. Derived from the Greek word *koinon*, "common," it refers to the things all citizens of a city share. A collection of individuals becomes a civic community because each citizen has some share of the tangible and intangible goods of the city. The city's wealth and prosperity, its safety and public order, its institutions and education, its architecture, music halls, and museums are all *koinon* goods.

Just as importantly, all citizens share in the common project of advancing the good of the city. Sailors, soldiers, and craftsmen each have their own specialized communities, which aim at limited goods. Sailors pursue the good of sailing together. Soldiers join together to better themselves as soldiers. Craftsmen form guilds to improve their craft. The city embraces and encompasses all these smaller communities. In the civic *koinonia*, each citizen and each smaller *koinonia* aims for the good of the *whole* city. Sailors pursue the good of sailing for the sake of finding new trade routes to enrich the city. Soldiers improve their fighting skills to defend the city. Craftsmen hone their skills for the sake of beautifying civic life.

When the New Testament writers use *koinonia*, they're pointing to the "civic" character of the church. The church is the city of God among the cities of men. Each member and congregation shares the common goods of the church, and each member and congregation contributes to the common good of the whole.

The city of man cannot realize this aspiration. No matter how rich a city is, its resources are limited. No matter how widely or equally shared its goods, some are excluded. In ancient cities, most of the residents of the city don't share in the *koinonia* of the city. Slaves, women, foreigners, and people of low birth aren't citizens. They contribute to the city but don't share in the common goods of the city. No city of man fully practices the customs of *koinonia*.

The church is able to achieve what the ancient city could

not achieve because her common things are genuinely common. What holds the church together is a common share in God Himself. The church is deeply unified because her members have the Spirit in common. The union of Jew and Gentile, of nation and tribe, isn't social, but Spiritual (1 Cor 1:9; 2 Cor 13:14). Every member receives the Spirit according to the measure of Christ's gift (Eph 4:7).

The goods of the church are inexhaustible. The Spirit is a river of life who never runs dry. Filled with the Spirit He receives from his Father, Jesus has an infinite supply of gifts. He'll never run out of gifted people to give to the church. The Father is the Giver of every good and perfect gift. The living God needs nothing from us. Precisely because He has no needs, He gives to us life and breath and all things (Acts 17:25). He's the only possible source of *koinonia* because He's the only possible source of unbounded generosity.

And the goods of the church are available to all. *All* members of the body share the work of building the body. The word for "common good" in 1 Corinthians 12:7 is *symphero*, "carrying together." In the church, *koinonia* isn't merely a *sharing*-together but a *bearing*-together, as each member uses the gifts he receives from the Spirit to edify the communion of believers, the body, Bride, and ark of Jesus (1 Cor 12:14–21). There are "master builders," and there are drones, but all edify the self-constructing ark of Jesus' body.

Eyes exist to serve all the sightless organs. Ears serve deaf eyes and mouth and hands and feet. Hands lend their manual power to the whole body. Eyes serve hands by directing the hands to things to touch and hold and avoid; hands serve eyes by shooing away bugs or putting on spectacles. It would be absurd for the eyes to become envious of the ears' power of hearing, or for the stomach to long to have *his own* feet. The body's feet *are* the stomach's feet; the body's ears are the ears of the eyes, as well as the ears of the nose, the tongue, the lungs, the muscles, the bones, the spleen. Each member of the body does his unique work for all the other members of the body. Each builds up the whole. Each serves each for the edification of the whole.

In Christ's body, *no* organ is vestigial. The parts that seem less honorable receive more abundant honor. Unpresentable members are adorned to become presentable. Despised, lowly, and weak members have their own special work to do in building up the body (1 Cor 12:22–26). Jesus gives capacities or abilities through His Spirit. Jesus gives *people* with Spiritual abilities or gifts: apostles, prophets, pastors, teachers, administrators, helpers, healers, secretaries, servants. In the church, there are no small gifts or small people. *Everyone* has the dignity of serving God in serving His house. All of us share in the work of building the ark of Jesus. "Administration" (1 Cor 12:28) doesn't seem as sexy as "prophecy" or "tongues" or gifts of healing, but it's no less necessary to the body. If you don't believe me, try running a church without a secretary.

Devotion to *koinonia* (Acts 2:42) includes holding all property in *koinon* (Acts 2:44; 4:34–37). Filled with the Spirit, the early Christians in Jerusalem sell their goods to help impoverished brothers and sisters. Material goods are like Spiritual goods. We receive everything we receive to edify the body and Bride, to build the ark of Jesus. And we receive *everything*. We possess our material property as we possess our Spiritual capacities, *as gifts* to be shared.

The church in Jerusalem has unique needs. Thousands join the church on a single day, and some need support. Besides, Jesus predicts Jerusalem will be destroyed. Christians don't have much incentive to invest in real estate within the holy city. With a flood coming to overwhelm Jerusalem, there's little reason to retain a portfolio of properties. Sale of land and houses is voluntary. When Ananias and Sapphira lie about their gift to the church,

Peter reminds them they could have kept their property if they had chosen (Acts 5:4).

But the custom of sharing goods isn't confined to Jerusalem. Jerusalem is the standard for all churches in all times and places. After all, the Jerusalem church isn't the only New Testament church where believers sacrifice their own wealth to build the body. Many of the New Testament's uses of *koinonia* refer to sharing material goods (Rom 15:26; 2 Cor 8:4; Heb 13:16). Because of the church's *koinonia* in material goods, the church fulfills the hopes of Israel (Deut 15:4): "there was not a needy person among them" (Acts 4:34).

Wealth might be used to build a business to employ others. A wealthy person might create a foundation to fund cultural or political projects. Wealth can be given away as charity. Whatever form it takes, wealth, like Spiritual gifts, is given for the sake of the body. Christian *koinonia* demands that each distributes to each as any has need (Acts 4:35). This is the custom of the church that builds the body.

Material *koinonia* serves Spiritual *koinonia*. Jews and Gentiles are united by the Spirit in Christ, but for Paul this union is realized by the sharing of goods—the Jews sharing their Spiritual goods with Gentiles, and Gentiles responding with funds for famine relief in Jerusalem (Rom 15:27). Macedonians make a *koinonia* contribution to poor saints in Jerusalem (Rom 15:26). As Paul sees it, they don't throw money at a problem from a distance. Rather, their generous gifts overcome distance, joining Macedonian Gentiles and Jerusalem Jews in one fellowship of the Spirit. Material gifts have a quasi-sacramental power to join the members of the church into one body. Charity is a tool for erecting the ark of the Carpenter of Nazareth.

In Acts 2, Luke uses a definite article: "*the koinonia*." He refers to an *event* of communion, not merely a quality or general practice of communion. The liturgy is that event of communion. In it, we gather to share together in Jesus and His Spirit. In the liturgy, we receive the teaching of the apostles, and we devote a portion of our goods to God and to one another. The Eucharist is a ritual expression of the *koinonia* of the church, which is also a *means* to realize that unity (1 Cor 10:16). In the liturgy, we share together in "*the* prayers" (Acts 2:42). Liturgy is at the center of the common life in Jesus' holy ark.

Gathered or dispersed, the church is always and everywhere a communion. But it manifests its *koinonia* to the world's powers particularly in its weekly gatherings on the Lord's Day. Then we join with the joyful assembly on the heavenly Zion, as the Spirit joins heaven and earth (Heb 12:22–24) so that we on earth can share the good things of the age to come.

Breaking Bread

Through baptism, Jesus gathers the lumber and workmen to build His people-ark and equips them with skill to make well. Through practices of communion, Jesus builds up His body. Through baptism and *koinonia*, *we* build the body and Bride of Christ. As we raise the edifice, we enjoy the abundant life of the kingdom at the Lord's table. Like Paul *en route* to Rome (Acts 27:33–36), Jesus gives thanks, breaks bread, and feeds the crew aboard His ark. Feasting is the work of the church.

Hosting a feast is hardly new for the Christ who comes "eating and drinking" (Luke 7:34). Luke records at least ten meals (Luke 5:27–39; 7:36–50; 9:10–17; 10:38–42; 11:37–54; 14:1–24; 19:1–10; 27:7–38; 24:13–35; 24:36–53), which symbolize Jesus' mission to preach good news to the poor and announce the favorable year of the Lord (Luke 4:16–30). In meals with Jesus, the poor and hungry are restored to the fat of the land.

Jesus forms a new Israel at His table. The people He eats with, often outcasts, are the first members of a new people of God.

Jesus cleanses the unclean. He purifies lepers, stops the flow of blood, raises the dead. He defeats the powers of death and impurity so He can welcome every penitent to His table. The meal is both a sign of the presence of the kingdom and a visible realization of that kingdom. Asked to point to the kingdom of God on earth, we should point to Jesus eating a meal with sinners.

For Jesus, table manners provide patterns for life. The virtues cultivated at the table are the virtues of the disciples. Jesus observes the competition among guests for important seats at the table (Luke 14:7). He rejects the honor game and commands His disciples to seek honor from God rather than from men. Jesus turns to the guest list (Luke 14:12) and warns against calculating hospitality (cf. Luke 6:30–35). We should imitate the hospitality of God, who gives generously even though we can never repay Him. Jesus doesn't consider repayment evil. Those who seek an invitation in payment for an invitation want too *little*, not too *much* (Luke 6:35). They seek a paltry reward in this age rather than the wealth of the age to come.

After the Spirit falls, the church continues on Jesus' table mission. Alongside *koinonia* in the Spirit and in goods, Jesus' disciples commune in bread (Acts 2:42). They break bread in the various house gatherings that spring up after Pentecost (Acts 2:46). At Ephesus, Paul gathers with the church on the first day of the week "to break bread" (Acts 20:7, 11). Paul teaches, but the purpose of the Sunday gathering isn't "to hear a sermon." The believers pray, but the purpose isn't to "pray together." The goal of gathering is to "break bread," to have a meal together. As Paul puts it elsewhere, Christians come together "to eat" (1 Cor 11:33).

Luke emphasizes *bread*, specifically *breaking* bread. You break a loaf to share it. But Jesus highlights another aspect of breaking. At the Last Supper, Jesus calls the bread His body, given for the disciples (Luke 22:19). Jesus is the bread broken in His trial

EDIFICATION

and death. After Pentecost, the church sees herself in the broken bread. Filled with the leaven of the Spirit, baked in fiery trials, the church *is* the bread of life, broken for the life of the world.

Throughout Acts, shared meals are evangelistic and edifying. They bring new members and groups into the *koinonia* of the church and continue the building project. Saul breathes out (*empneuo*) threats and murder against the church (Acts 9:1) until Jesus confronts him and turns him from a persecutor into a persecuted apostle. In Damascus, he's baptized and filled with the Spirit (*pneuma*, Acts 9:17) and shares a meal with his former enemy (Acts 9:19). Saul becomes a table companion to those he once tried to destroy.

When Cornelius's servants arrive at Simon's house, Peter and Simon welcome them and show hospitality, feeding the strangers and spending the night under the same roof (Acts 10:23). When Peter returns with them to Caesarea, he remains a few days (Acts 10:48), sharing a house and a table. This is the aim of the gospel: to overcome distance, to break down the dividing wall between Jew and Gentile, slave and free, male and female, to clothe all with Christ so all can share the table of Jesus.

Common meals aren't mere "symbols" of *koinonia*. They're acts of *koinonia* that encompass acts of charity. The first internal conflict of the early church has to do with inequitable distribution of food. Hellenistic Jewish widows complain that the Hebrew widows are being favored in the "daily serving of food" (Acts 6:1). The apostles instruct the church to select six men to oversee the "serving of tables" (Acts 6:2). Within weeks of Pentecost, the church has its own rudimentary charity system where food is distributed to those without means to support themselves. Later, when famine threatens Judea, the common table expands beyond Jerusalem to encompass the empire. Each gives according to his means to relieve the saints in famine-ridden Jerusalem (Acts 11:27–30). Scattered as they are throughout the empire, the church feasts at a single table.

The shared meal is the biblical paradigm of Christian charity. At the table, those with goods share them with those who have none. Rich and poor share bread *together* and so also share time, conversation, burdens, laughter, tears, life. Whatever charity work the church engages in, it should take the common table as a paradigm.

A church isn't carrying out the mission of Jesus if it doesn't gather on the Lord's Day at a common table. A weekly Eucharist is a minimum. A church isn't carrying out the mission of Jesus if it doesn't hospitably welcome former enemies to break bread. A church isn't carrying out the mission of Jesus if it shuns outsiders, treats them as unclean, and refuses to eat together. A church isn't carrying out the mission of Jesus if it doesn't excommunicate impenitent sinners. A church isn't carrying out the mission of Jesus unless it serves tables, cares for its own widows and orphans, contributes to relieve the needs of brothers and sisters on the other side of the world.

Jesus ministers at tables. His church carries on His mission to the world by continuing His table work. Within His ark-temple, His disciples enjoy a continuous feast.

The Prayers

Common prayer is the clearest custom of the perfected *koinonia* of the church. Ancient Greek cities boasted of their democratic politics. Each citizen had a voice in public assembly. But many weren't citizens and so were voteless and voiceless. In the church, *everyone* has a voice. Every member is in Christ, and so all share the same status before the Father. All are filled with the one Spirit who intercedes for us. No voices are drowned out. The least and lowest has as much right to be heard as the high and honored. At prayer, the church is, as Robert Jenson put it, a perfect participatory democracy.

The church's mission is saturated with prayer. Before the Spirit falls at Pentecost, the disciples are "continuously devoted to prayer" (Acts 1:14). Throughout Acts, the apostles and churches pray before they set apart leaders of the church (Acts 1:24). Through prayer and the laying on of hands, the apostles commission six men to carry on table service to the widows of Jerusalem (Acts 6:6). By prayer and fasting, the church at Antioch sets apart Paul and Barnabas for their mission to the Gentiles (Acts 13:3). When Paul visits established churches, he prays and appoints elders to carry on the work he started (Acts 14:23).

Prayer is one of the church's weapons for combatting death and disease. Peter prays to raise Tabitha from the dead (Acts 9:40), and Saul prays in Damascus after his life-altering encounter with Jesus (Acts 9:11). Paul prays and lays hands on the father of Publius to heal him (Acts 28:8).

Prayer is also a shield and a city wall. When the apostles come under attack, their first response is to pray. When the Jewish establishment in Jerusalem arrests and tries Peter and John, the church offers a remarkable prayer (Acts 4:24–29). They appeal to the Creator using words from Psalm 146 (cf. Acts 14:15) and then quote the opening verses of Psalm 2. The Jews of Jerusalem have become raging Gentiles who gather against the Lord and His Christ. They've done it before, when they joined with Pilate and the Gentiles in opposing Jesus. Now they're doing it again, attacking the body of Christ.

The whole prayer is premised on the instruction Jesus gave the Eleven during the forty days after the resurrection: They've learned to see the Scriptures as the story of Jesus, *and* they've learned to see their own lives embedded within the story of Jesus. They ask God to "take note of their threats," to silence their accusers. They ask the Davidic King who reigns from Zion with an iron rod to dash His enemies like pottery. In the face of threats, the church doesn't pray for rescue or relief. They pray for boldness in speech and receive a renewed filling of the Spirit, who loosens their tongues for witness (Acts 4:31). Their prayers literally shake the land.

Paul and Silas's prayers and songs shake Philippi and open the prison doors (Acts 16:25). The incident is so impressive that the jailer asks how he can be saved, and their prayers humble the magistrates who put them in prison in the first place. When Peter is sent to prison, prayers spring him out too (Acts 12:5). Against the prayers of the church, no enemy can stand. No jail can hold a praying and singing church. If the prison doors stay closed, the prison itself becomes a temple filled with prayer and praise. Jesus keeps building His human ark even when His crew is in custody.

Paul's and Silas's song in the Philippian jail is the only reference to Psalm-singing in the book of Acts. Yet the frequent quotations show that the early church was deeply familiar with the Psalter (Acts 1:20; 2:25–28, 34–35; 4:25–28; 7:46; 13:33, 35; 14:15). Paul makes clear that singing is a gift of the Spirit. Don't be drunk with wine, Paul writes, but be filled with the Spirit, who inspires psalms, hymns, Spiritual songs, and melodies in the heart (Eph 5:18–19). In song and prayer, the church shakes the world and brings down principalities and powers.

Many prayers in Acts are occasional, tied to specific needs and occasions. But Acts 2:42 suggests something more. The baptized were devoted to the apostles' teaching, to *koinonia*, to the breaking of bread, and "to *the* prayers." The noun is plural, and it's preceded by the definite article, "the." These prayers are occasional or spontaneous. The early disciples follow a form of prayer, a liturgical order of prayer that guides collective prayers during the church's gatherings. It's not surprising that the apostles continue to observe the hours of temple prayer and sometimes pray in the temple (Acts 2:46; 3:1; 10:9, 30). In Philippi, Lydia initially joins a group of Jews and God-fearers praying outside the walls of the city (Acts 16:13, 16). After Paul and Silas leave the city, Lydia's house *within* the city walls becomes the center of prayer. Every church Paul starts is a prayer meeting. The church's communion in prayer is *liturgical* communion in prayer.

Conclusion

The Carpenter of Nazareth comes to remake creation, but His first task is to construct an ark made of people, which He makes *through* the people. We're a self-forming body, a self-edifying ark, both material and builders. We're God's workmanship (*poiema*, a made-thing), but He completes His *poiema* through us (Eph 2:10) as we keep the customs of the apostles. The church is the greatest artifact of man the maker, the greatest artwork of the Last Adam and His body. It's breathtaking to realize we share in this project. But it's just what we expect from a Creator who creates by giving creatures power to create, a Maker who makes man a maker.

This task is foundational, but it's not the final task. The ultimate task is to bring the world into the ark, to remake the cities of men to resemble the city of God.

4 PILOT

We must run aground on a certain island.
Acts 27:26

Luke's account of Paul's life and ministry can seem like a geography lesson, and a confusing one. After his breach with Barnabas, he travels through Syria and Cilicia, then to Derbe and Lystra, Phrygia and the Galatian region, and finally to Troas, where he receives a vision instructing him to move on to Macedonia (Acts 15:41—16:2, 6–10). Sprung from a Philippian jail, he journeys through Amphipolis and Apollonia to Thessalonica (Acts 17:1). As Paul makes his way to Jerusalem, he takes a farewell tour of the churches, from Ephesus through Macedonia to Philippi to Troas, then to Assos and Mitylene and, having crossed to Samos, to Miletus (Acts 20:1–6, 13–15).

Got it?

Luke is recording history, but he's doing more. He's showing the Scriptures fulfilled in the suffering and glory of Christ and in the suffering and glory of the apostles. Paul resembles the original traveler, the peripatetic Abraham, who leaves Ur for Haran

(Gen 11:27–32) and then, commanded by Yahweh, moves from Haran to the land of Canaan (Gen 12:1–5). He doesn't settle for long. At Shechem, Yahweh appears to him, and Abraham builds a commemorative altar (Gen 12:6–7). Then he moves east of Bethel to build another altar (Gen 12:8), before moving south to the Negev (Gen 12:9), then to Egypt to escape a famine (Gen 12:10–20). When he returns, he still doesn't stay put. Yahweh appears to him at the "oaks of Moreh" near Shechem (Gen 12:6–7), and he later moves on to a site between Kadesh and Shur, becoming a resident alien in Gerar (Gen 20:1–20).

Genesis isn't a mere travelogue any more than Acts. Abraham is heir of the land, and his travels are a "walk-through" of his descendants' inheritance. As Yahweh tells Joshua, "Every place on which the sole of your foot treads, I have given it to you" (Josh 1:3; cf. Deut 11:24). Joshua conquers and takes possession of the land because Abraham has pre-conquered it by erecting altars to Yahweh throughout Canaan. Joshua wins battles at places where Abraham built altars. First worship, then conquest.

The other great travelogue in the Old Testament is Israel's itinerary through the wilderness. Israel leaves Egypt on the way to the land of promise, camping along the way. When they get to Mount Hor, Aaron dies (Num 20:22–29; cf. Num 33:38), and Israel immediately begins the conquest, defeating the king of Arad (Num 21:1–3), Sihon (Num 21:21–25), and Og (Num 21:33–35; cf. Psa 135:11; 136:20). Numbers 33 plots the journey in great detail.

Paul is an apostle of the God of Abraham, who is, Paul says, "heir of the world" (Rom 4:13). He's an ambassador of the High King of heaven and earth, a member of Christ's body. Wherever he goes, Christ goes. Wherever he proclaims, Christ claims. Paul builds living temples throughout the Eastern Mediterranean, filled with living images of the living God. His foot treads around Syria, Asia Minor, Greece, and eventually to Rome because King Jesus lays claim to these lands and peoples.

Paul's travels are also a passage through the wilderness as he approaches the "promised land" of Jerusalem, capital of Judaism, and then Rome, capital of the Gentile world. Both are Jerichoes, whose walls will fall before a greater Joshua. The promise to Joshua applies to Paul: Every place his foot treads is given to him.

Halfway through Acts, Paul becomes a sailor, and we get another travelogue. He sails from Troas to Macedonia, from Macedonia to Miletus, from Miletus to Caesarea and Jerusalem. From Jerusalem, he returns to Caesarea, where he begins his long, turbulent voyage to Rome. Abraham and Joshua were landlubbers, tracing the contours of the land of promise. Like Jesus, Paul can stride the waves. He measures out the Gentile sea, claiming it as the holy dwelling place of the God of earth and ocean, claiming the world for the Greater Noah.

Acts ends with a long sea yarn. Paul's voyage to Rome is an allegory of the aims and trajectory of Christian mission (Acts 27:1—28:16). His journey is a new exodus as he crosses water from Jerusalem, the new Egypt, toward Rome, the great city of the empire. He moves from the land of Israel through the Gentile sea. The ship is a fairly obvious symbol of the Roman ship of state. Paul sets sail in a Roman ship as a Roman prisoner, under custody to a centurion named Julius, who is from the Augustan battalion (Julius! Augustan!), who treats him with consideration (Acts 27:3).

Against Paul's advice, Julius sets out from Fair Havens and immediately runs into a turbulent storm. The sky turns apocalyptic; darkness blots out sun and stars (Acts 27:20). It's another Deluge. A world is coming to an end, and the Roman ship of state is sure to be wrecked. During the storm, Paul effectively becomes the ship's captain. He assures the crew that no one will be lost (Acts 27:21–26) and orders the sailors to stay on the ship (Acts 27:30–32), while Julius prevents the soldiers from killing the prisoners because of his determination to bring Paul to Rome (Acts 27:42–43).

On the morning of the fourteenth day after Yom Kippur (Acts 27:9, 27, 33), Paul encourages the crew to eat. He takes bread, gives thanks, breaks it, and passes it out to the 276 on board (Acts 27:35–37). He turns the Roman ship into a church, the site of Eucharist. He's another Jonah who leads a ship's crew to worship the living God while traveling to preach in a city threatened with destruction.

A skilled workman in the company of the Carpenter of Nazareth, Paul measures not only the church but the world, in anticipation that both the land of Israel and the sea of Rome will be brought into the ark of Christendom, dry and safe. This is what Paul is after from the outset. He doesn't intend merely to rescue a few from the shipwreck. He and the other apostles aim to save *everyone* and to pilot the Roman ship safely through the storms of coming judgment. He intends to overthrow the powers and replace the sacrifices to demons with the Eucharistic sacrifice. As an apostle of the Greater Noah, he pilots a new ark that will bring the voyagers to a new world.

Acts is an incomplete story. The final chapters anticipate Paul's trial in Rome, as the gospels anticipate Jesus' trial in Jerusalem. But when Acts ends, Paul is still under house arrest, preaching the gospel and awaiting his hearing before Caesar. Luke's open non-ending is deliberate. Acts is unfinished because the history Luke records is unfinished. Paul completes his inspection of the Roman world. He has finished his walk-through. Rome is ripe for Jesus' conquest. But there are worlds elsewhere.

Over the centuries, others pick up where Paul ends, walking through other lands of Abraham's inheritance—through Armenia and India, China and Japan, the Near East and the Far East, the Americas and Oceania and the islands of the sea. We're still walking. Every land where the feet of Christ's body tread belongs to the Seed of Abraham, heir of the world. We claim every sea we traverse as His realm. Wherever Jesus builds temples, everywhere *we* build temples, Jesus lays His claim. Wherever we sail, Jesus builds His saving vessel. Jesus sends us to take charge of the world and to pilot the nations toward fair havens.

Proclamation to Powers

When the flood destroyed all flesh, Noah's ark saved eight persons. In the first century, a flood threatens to sweep away the world as ancients know it. The Carpenter of Nazareth makes an ark big enough to carry the world over the waves onto dry land, where the world can be born again. The church's mission is never simply a rescue operation, snatching a few sinners from Satan's claws or from the fires of hell. The church's mission is a conquest. She aims to disciple the nations so they become the inheritance of the Christ and His Bride.

We accomplish this by proclaiming and enacting the mystery. God unveils His manifold wisdom to rulers and authorities in heavenly places through the church (Eph 3:9–10). A "mystery" is something hidden in God for ages past and now revealed in Christ. In Ephesians, the mystery is the union of Jews and Gentiles in the one body of Jesus, the good news that Gentiles are "fellow heirs and fellow members of the body, and fellow partakers of the promise" (Eph 3:4–6). A unified humanity: *This* is the truth we proclaim to the powers.

Principalities are Babelic. They obliterate differences and force unity. Or, they exploit division by deepening the chasm between masters and slaves, by turning the fruitful created difference of male and female into a structure of oppression or envy, by protecting the unjust wealth of the wicked wealthy and justifying indifference to the poor, by twisting the healthy diversity of languages and cultures into mutual hatred.

As the one body, the church demonstrates that fleshly

markers of division have been overcome in the resurrection of Jesus. Masters and slaves continue to exist, but masters treat slaves as brothers and slaves live as freemen in Christ. Men and women are reconciled in one flesh by the Spirit. The wealthy open their hands so that the poor have enough to share. People from every tribe, tongue, and nation are bound by mutual exchanges of Spiritual and material goods.

The mystery isn't perfectly realized in the church. Christian masters are cruel, Christian husbands and wives abuse one another, rich Christians hoard wealth, and poor Christians become envious and resentful. National hatreds divide the church. Yet the mystery *does* become visible, and when it doesn't, the Word, Spirit, and Sacraments continually call the church to repentance, to exhibit the mystery more fully.

For all the church's blemishes, her sheer existence exposes the lie of rulers and authorities, the lie that social order requires division and domination. The church proclaims this: There's another game in town, another civic order within the city of man. *There is an alternative.* Every time the church celebrates Eucharist, or gathers donations for victims of a natural catastrophe on the other side of the world, or reconciles warring tribes, it brings the mystery to light. It makes known the wisdom of God to the rulers and authorities. Every time the church exhibits *koinonia*, she demonstrates the rulers and authorities are powerless. Every faithful act of the church shakes the foundations of the world and brings some plot of earth into the ark of Jesus.

Defeating the Devil

Jesus is Prince of Peace. He will reconcile heaven and earth and bring peace to earth. The road to peace is, inevitably, a road of conflict and suffering. The road to new life for the world runs past Golgotha.

THEOPOLITAN MISSION

The church continues Jesus' warfare against Satan and his demons. Jesus' ministry begins with His baptism, quickly followed by forty days of temptation in the wilderness (Matt 3:13—4:11; Mark 1:12-13; Luke 3:21—4:12). The devil tempts Jesus to prove Himself Son of God by turning stones to bread, by throwing Himself from the temple tower, by bowing to Satan. In each case, Jesus responds with Scripture: "Man doesn't live by bread alone," and "You shall worship the Lord your God and serve Him only," and "You shall not put the Lord your God to the test." Jesus is the true Israel, resisting temptations in the wilderness. He's the Last Adam, driven into the cursed desert to do battle with the serpent.

Jesus conquers the devil in the wilderness, then embarks on the mission of overthrowing Satan's kingdom. He exorcizes a demon from a man who confronts Him in a synagogue (Mark 1:21-28). In the country of the Gerasenes lives a man possessed by a Legion of demons. He's too strong for anyone to bind, a zombie living among the tombs. Jesus casts the Legion into a herd of pigs, which charge into the water and drown (Mark 5:1-20). He delivers the daughter of a Syrophoenician woman (Matt 15:21-28; Mark 7:24-30), a blind and mute man (Matt 12:22-32; Mark 3:20-30; Luke 11:14-23), and a boy whose demon throws him into water and fire (Matt 17:14-21; Mark 9:14-29; Luke 9:37-49). He establishes a house of healing, where He heals diseases and casts out demons (Matt 8:16-17; Mark 1:32-34; Luke 4:40-41).

Jesus is the Stronger Man who binds Satan, the strong man, and plunders his house (Matt 12:29; Mark 3:27; Luke 11:21). Even if Jesus' enemies are right and He casts out demons by the power of Satan, His exorcisms are still a sign of Satan's impending defeat. Once Satan starts casting out Satan, his kingdom is divided and about to fall (Matt 12:24-26).

Jesus' exorcisms dramatize the arrival of the kingdom. If He casts out demons by the finger-Spirit of God, the kingdom of God has come upon Israel (Matt 12:28; Luke 11:20). Pharaoh's magicians recognized Yahweh's Finger in the plagues (Exod 8:19), but the blinded Jews can't see the divine Finger when it pokes them in the eye. Jesus has Satan on the run. Especially in His death, He drives the "ruler of this world" from the field (cf. John 12:31–32). This is what the coming of the kingdom means: God overthrows His enemies and wrests back control of His world.

That is what Jesus began to do and teach (Acts 1:1). After the apostles receive the Spirit-finger at Pentecost, Jesus continues His warfare through them. They preach and heal and drive out demons. Paul exorcises a "spirit of divination" from a slave girl in Philippi (Acts 16:16–18). More typically, the apostles don't encounter Satan or demons directly. They battle Satanically inspired people. Peter says Satan drove Ananias to lie to the Holy Spirit (Acts 5:3), and Paul denounces Bar-Jesus or Elymas as a "son of the devil" (Acts 13:10). Paul's entire mission is a deliverance, calling Jews and Gentiles from darkness to light and from the dominion of Satan to God (Acts 26:18).

The entire church is enlisted into the host that battles Satan. Our battle is against "principalities and powers" and Spiritual forces in heavenly places (Eph 6:12). Peter warns that the devil prowls like a lion seeking prey (1 Pet 5:8), and James says hell-fire can inspire our speech (Jas 3:6). Once Paul establishes churches, he feels responsible to preserve them from Satanic seduction. He compares the Corinthians to Eve and himself to a servant of the Last Adam, who guards the Bride from the serpent (2 Cor 11:3).

When Jesus pulls back the veil, John sees the demonic powers behind the church's human enemies. Jews who oppose the Messiah become "synagogues of Satan" (Rev 2:9; 3:9), false teachers in Thyatira urge believers to penetrate the "deep things of Satan" (Rev 2:24), and Pergamum is the place "where Satan's throne is" (Rev 2:13). Once the dragon is tossed from heaven

(Rev 12:1–12), he pursues the Bride and her children (Rev 12:13–17) and then calls up monsters from the sea and land to overcome the saints (Rev 13:1–18). Inspired by the dragon, Romans and Jews ally together against the church.

In Revelation, Babylon represents Jerusalem, the city that drinks the blood of the prophets and saints (Rev 18:24; cf. Matt 23:35). She's a harlot and a sorceress (Rev 18:23), and she's not the only one. In Samaria, Philip encounters Simon Magus, a prophet and magician who is baptized and joins the church. When he sees Peter and John confer the Spirit, he offers to pay to learn the trick. Peter rebukes him severely (Acts 8:9–24). Paul's impact on Ephesus is even more dramatic. Ephesus is the climax of Paul's Gentile mission. He stays three years, until "all who lived in Asia heard the word of the Lord" (Acts 19:10). His success provokes opposition. Demetrius the silversmith objects that "not only in Ephesus but in almost all of Asia, this Paul has persuaded and turned a considerable number of people" from idols (Acts 19:26).

Paul's exorcisms are so successful that unbelieving Jews start imitating him. Seven sons of the Jewish priest Sceva attempt to exorcise a demon-possessed man with the words, "I adjure you by Jesus whom Paul preaches" (Acts 19:13). The demon knows Jesus and Paul but doesn't recognize these exorcists. The man is as powerful as the Gadarene demoniac, pouncing on the Scevans and driving them away wounded and naked (Acts 19:13–16). When the news spreads through Ephesus, many acknowledge the power of Jesus, before whom even the demons bow. He's Lord of demons, who takes away the potency of magical practices. Like one of the cities of Canaan under the ban, Ephesus becomes the site of a conflagration as the residents burn fifty thousand silver pieces' worth of magical books (Acts 19:19). Paul's signs and wonders surpass magic. The Word of the Lord is more powerful than any incantation. Jesus has overcome the prince of this world, and the world ruled by that fallen prince won't survive for long.

War on Mammon

Mammon is one of the chief powers of the world, one of the primary idols against which Jesus and the church wage war. Jesus preaches an economically-charged gospel. In the synagogue of Nazareth, Jesus introduces Himself as the Servant of Yahweh prophesied by Isaiah. Filled with the Spirit, the Servant preaches good news to the poor, release to captives, sight to the blind, and rescue for the downtrodden (Luke 4:16–21; cf. Isa 61:1–2). Jesus announces a great Jubilee, which brings release to slaves and a restoration of Israel to the land (cf. Lev 25).

Throughout His public life, Jesus confronts the powerful wealthy with a call to sacrificial generosity. "Woe to you who are rich," He says, and "woe to you who are well-fed." The time is coming when the rich will no longer be comforted, when the well-fed will be left hungry (Luke 6:24-25). Jesus targets the Jerusalem elites, who combine wealth with political clout. The parable of the good Samaritan contrasts priests and Levites, finicky about purity, with the Samaritan who proves himself a good neighbor to the man who was robbed (Luke 10:25–37). The rich man in the parable of Lazarus is dressed like a priest, in purple and fine linen, and lives in splendor and festivity (Luke 16:19–31). Jesus doesn't condemn wealth, but He eviscerates ungenerous temple elites, who devour widows' houses and ignore the ulcerated beggars sitting at the gates of the temple. Nothing raises His ire like abuse of the weak.

The parable of the unjust steward ends with Jesus' observation that possessions ("mammon") should be used to "make friends" so that one can be received into eternal dwellings (Luke 16:1–13). The steward, wicked as he is (Luke 16:8), knows what money is for: Money is not to be worshiped or hoarded. It's not a lord or god (Luke 16:13). Money is for making friends. The only question is what friends we're trying to make. Do we make friends with powerful elites, or do we make friends with God by making friends with the poor?

As soon as the Spirit falls on the disciples, they continue the Servant's mission, including His war on Mammon. Like Jesus, they preach the gospel to the poor, release to prisoners, liberty to the oppressed. The three thousand disciples begin to sell their possessions to provide for needy brothers. In Acts 6, the church sets up a system of charity to care for widows. They faithfully break bread together and—as Jew and Gentile, Parthian and Mede and Elamite, Cretan and Arab—sit at a common table. By their *koinonia* in material goods, Christians proclaim the mystery. By their generosity, they announce Jesus' victory over Mammon.

Mammon's worshipers don't want to hear the news. Ananias and Sapphira keep back part of the proceeds of the sale of their property. They give the illusion of generosity without suffering any loss; they're greedy both for money and for a reputation for giving away their money (Acts 5:1–11). In Philippi, Paul's accusers are riled when Paul drives a spirit of divination from a slave girl. As soon as the demon "comes out," they see their hope of profit "coming out" (Acts 16:18–19). In Ephesus, Demetrius whips the silversmiths into a riotous froth by reminding them how much they're liable to lose if Paul's message about idols takes hold (Acts 19:23–27). Greed infects the rulers who judge Paul. Felix keeps Paul in prison in Caesarea because he wants a bribe (Acts 24:26). The enemies of Jesus and Paul are all lovers of money (cf. Luke 16:14), and so are ours. Throughout the ages, the church suffers persecution when she dares to confront the powerful who get fat by devouring the poor.

Demetrius and the owners of the slave girl are entrepreneurs of religion, using religion as a cover for greed. When their wealth is threatened, they respond violently, but deceptively, with a show of public-spirited concern for the common good. "These men are throwing our city into confusion," say the Philippian slave-owners (Acts 16:20). Artemis is being "dethroned from her magnificence," says Demetrius (Acts 19:27). In a sense, they're right. Philippi and Ephesus are ordered by worship of Mammon, and Paul challenges the foundations of society when he takes away their idols. The apostles wouldn't be the least surprised by today's surfeit of religious kitsch, our multi-millionaire preachers, or the contemporary uses of God-speak to conceal envy and covetousness. Money continues to corrupt the faith, and it's the church's mission to obliterate Mammon's reign in the church as much as in the world.

Paul's own practices stand in sharp contrast. When he stays for a long time in Corinth, he finds work as a tent-maker (Acts 18:1–3). At Ephesus, he works with his hands to meet his own needs (Acts 20:34). He can say without pretense, "I have coveted no one's silver or gold or clothes" (Acts 20:33) because he has followed Jesus' instruction: "It is more blessed to give than to receive" (Acts 20:35). Paul learns the lesson of the parable of the steward: He uses Mammon to make friends with the poor and hence with God.

Money forges a friendship between Jews and Gentiles. As he travels from Gentile church to Gentile church, Paul raises funds to carry back to Jerusalem as famine relief. Gentiles have become "partakers" (*koinoneo*) of the Jews' Spiritual goods and should respond by sharing material goods (Rom 15:27). Like the table fellowship where Jew and Gentile share bread (see Gal 2:11–14), money breaks down the dividing wall and forms one new humanity. Money forms a communion in mission. As an apostle, Paul "sows" Spiritual goods among the churches (1 Cor 9:11), and he expects to reap a harvest when the Corinthians help him with donations. Out of this sowing and reaping, Paul's communion with the churches deepens. The Philippians share (*sugkoinoneo*) both Paul's affliction and his work as they commune (*koinoneo*) with him in "giving and receiving" (Phil 4:15).

In the market, money causes a *break* of fellowship. We pay the clerk or waiter, and we don't have to have any further dealings with him. We don't *want* to buy friendship, only goods and services. The gospel radically transforms our notion of money and its uses. Not only in the church but also in the marketplace, money is a sign and seal of personal communion. The hippies were right: Money is bread, like the *Eucharistic* bread that serves as an effective sign of the communion of giver and receiver in the mission of Jesus and in His Spirit. The economy of the church is a Eucharistic economy, and the church is called to pilot the world economy away from the shoals of Mammon into the safe haven of *koinonia*.

The Powers Strike Back

Everywhere Jesus goes, He provokes opposition. So do His disciples. Peter and John heal a man who has been lame from birth (Acts 3:1–10). While Peter preaches to the amazed crowd, the captain of the temple guard seizes them and takes them to prison (Acts 4:1–4). Later, they perform signs and wonders in Solomon's portico, and the high priest again arrests and imprisons them (Acts 5:12–18). When an angel leads them from the prison, they don't take a break or skip town. They head straight back to the temple to start preaching again (Acts 5:21–22). This time, the Sanhedrin flogs them and orders them to stop talking about Jesus (Acts 5:40–41).

Opposition escalates. After Stephen's death, the Jews begin a systematic, officially sponsored persecution. Saul pursues Christians from house to house, arresting and imprisoning both men and women (Acts 8:1-3). He tortures them to blaspheme Jesus, and he casts his vote to put them to death (Acts 26:10-11). Herod puts James to death and imprisons Peter (Acts 12).

Arrest and warning. Arrest and imprisonment. Then arrest and beating. Then a mob execution. Then systematic persecution. The conflict escalates and doesn't stop when Paul converts. On the contrary, the chief persecutor becomes the persecuted.

While Paul is still in Damascus, Jews plot to kill him. The disciples help him escape through a window in the city wall (Acts 9:23-25), like the spies from Rahab's house (Josh 2:15-21) or a new David (1 Sam 19:11-17). When Jews at Pisidian Antioch become jealous of Paul's success, they contradict him and blaspheme Jesus (Acts 13:44-46). At Iconium, the Jews again oppose Paul and attempt to stone him to death (Acts 14:4-6).

Like Paul himself in his earlier life, the Jews move from city to city, carrying on an anti-mission. Jews from Antioch and Iconium stone Paul and drag him out of Lystra, leaving him for dead (Acts 14:19-20). Everywhere, Paul is accused, beaten, arrested, and imprisoned. No wonder Paul speaks like a madman (2 Cor 11:23) and boasts of his sufferings: beatings, stonings, shipwrecks, journeys, dangers from rivers, robbers, Jews, Gentiles, threats in the city and in the wilderness and among false brothers (2 Cor 11:23-27).

Conflict is no accident, nor is it avoidable. Suffering is the only path into the kingdom, an inevitable part of mission. If you want a painless and comfortable life, it's best not to board the ark of a crucified Savior. Peter and John rejoice they are worthy to suffer for Jesus (Acts 5:41). Paul boasts of his brand-marks because his scars are physical evidence that he shares in Christ's sufferings for the sake of the church (Col 1:24). There's no mission without the cross. The church must be as crucifiable as her Lord. Jesus' self-building ark is constructed from the wood of a cross.

Advisor to the King

The apostolic mission is Spiritual war. It's also, at the same time, political combat. The apostles don't carry out their mission in the catacombs or retreat into secret intentional communities. They preach and act in public, in synagogues and town squares. Naturally, they end up in public squabbles with Jews and Gentiles who don't want Jesus to take over public life.

The Spirit and political battlefields overlap so much that they become indistinguishable. In Philippi, Paul expels a spirit of divination from a slave girl. Deprived of their livelihood, the girl's owners drag Paul and Silas to the magistrates, charging them with attacking the customs of the proudly Roman colony of Philippi. The mob and the magistrates strip the missionaries and beat them with rods, and the city leaders throw them into prison (Acts 16:16–24).

Overnight, an earthquake shakes the prison open, which leads to the conversion of the jailer and his household. The next morning, the humbled magistrates offer to let Paul and Silas leave town quietly, but Paul refuses. He suddenly reveals he's a Roman citizen and reminds the magistrates that they've permitted him to be beaten and imprisoned without trial. Paul wants the magistrates to admit their error in person (Acts 16:35–39). Paul demands a vindication as public as the violation.

Paul's demand has long-term effects. If the magistrates of Philippi allow Paul and Silas to preach, they'll also tolerate the group of believers gathered at Lydia's house (Acts 16:40). Paul wins a legal and political skirmish, but he achieves far more. He leaves behind a new Philippi, which now tolerates a church that teaches a subversive Way that, by the Philippians' own admission, "it is not lawful for us to accept or to observe, being Romans" (Acts 16:21). The mere existence of a Christian community in Philippi forces the city to alter public norms. Jesus builds

His ark in Philippi, and the city begins to clamor aboard.

The apostles' triumphs over false prophets, magicians, and idolaters are also political victories. In Samaria, Peter and John lay hands on believers to confer the Spirit. Simon, a magician who "claimed to be someone great" and is known as "the Great Power of God," offers to pay the apostles to teach him the trick. Peter severely rebukes Simon for his bondage to iniquity and the "gall of bitterness" (Acts 8:9–24). Simon, recognizing a power greater than his own, pleads with the apostles for forgiveness. You can bet Simon lost some prestige among the Samaritans after that incident. You can bet the apostles gained status. Exotic messengers from Judea who win power battles with magicians and prophets are a political force to be reckoned with.

Paul's confrontation with Bar-Jesus at Salamis is of particular note. At the beginning, Bar-Jesus is "with the proconsul, Sergius Paulus" (Acts 13:6–7), a court magician and prophet, like the magicians of Pharaoh or the prophets of Ahab. When Paul rebukes Bar-Jesus as a "son of the devil," Sergius Paulus is impressed: "the proconsul believed . . . being amazed at the teaching of the Lord" (Acts 13:12). A Roman proconsul named Paulus stops taking advice from one Jew in order to listen to his namesake.

In Luke's Gospel, Jesus' first sermon at Nazareth anticipates His entire mission as Isaiah's Spirit-anointed Servant of Yahweh (Luke 4:14–30). Set at the beginning of Paul's first missionary journey, the story of Bar-Jesus and Sergius Paulus previews his whole mission. The apostle to the Gentiles prevails over false teachers so Roman officials will submit to the teaching of the Lord. Paul takes over as advisor to the king. From the beginning of his mission, Paul is on his way to becoming the pilot of the Roman ship.

It's nothing new. When Israel is sown into Babylonian exile, Jeremiah instructs them to seek the peace of the city where they're sent (Jer 29). Jeremiah's instruction continues to apply after Persia defeats Babylon, after Alexander the Great defeats Persia, and after Rome conquers the Mediterranean world. As the Jews pursue the peace and good of the city of man, the Lord places some in high office. At the beginning of Israel's history, the Lord sends Joseph into Egypt ahead of Jacob and his sons. Pharaoh sets Joseph over the land of Egypt (Gen 41:41) to oversee the famine relief program. By the time Joseph's brothers arrive, Yahweh has prepared a place for them.

Yahweh does the same when Nebuchadnezzar threatens Judah. Daniel and his friends are taken to Babylon in the first deportation. By the time Nebuchadnezzar destroys the temple and the city, Daniel is already ruler of the province of Babylon and chief of the company of wise men (Dan 2:46–49). No wonder Jeremiah feels confident enough to urge the kings of Judah to surrender to Nebuchadnezzar. They have a friend in the highest place. When Persia overthrows Babylon, Daniel again rises to a high position, as one of the three commissioners over the 120 satraps of the Persian empire (Dan 6:1–2). Other Jews are highly placed in Persia too. Nehemiah is cupbearer to the king (Neh 1:11), Ezra is well-known as a scribe (Ezra 7:1–26), Esther becomes queen, and Mordecai ends up as the second to King Ahasuerus (Est 10:1–3).

These elite Jews are effective witnesses. Yahweh sends bad dreams to Pharaoh, sparking a series of events that elevates Joseph. Nebuchadnezzar too has a perplexing dream, which Daniel, a new Joseph, interprets (Dan 2). The Lord sends another dream in which a tree representing Nebuchadnezzar is cut down. Nebuchadnezzar is humbled and lives as a wild beast for a time before his human sanity is restored (Dan 4). In each case, the dreaming ruler ends up confessing the power of the God of Israel. Pharaoh recognizes a spirit of God in Joseph, which allows him to foresee the future (Gen 41:38–39). Nebuchadnezzar's confessions are among the most remarkable in Scripture:

"Surely your God is a God of gods and a Lord of kings and a revealer of mysteries, since you have been able to reveal this mystery" (Dan 2:47).

"I blessed the Most High and praised and honored Him who lives forever; for His dominion is an everlasting dominion, and His kingdom endures from generation to generation. And all the inhabitants of the earth are accounted as nothing, but He does according to His will in the host of heaven and among the inhabitants of earth; and no one can ward off His hand or say to Him, 'What hast Thou done?'" (Dan 4:34–35).

When interpreting Nebuchadnezzar's dream of the tree, Daniel rebukes the king not only about his pride, but also about the injustice of his reign: "break away now from your sins by doing righteousness, and from your iniquities by showing mercy to the poor, in case there may be a prolonging of your prosperity" (Dan 4:27). We aren't told what changes Nebuchadnezzar makes when he recovers, but we can guess he takes Daniel's warning seriously. He acknowledges Yahweh's dominion and kingdom. We can surmise that the chastened emperor seeks to conform his own kingdom to Yahweh's justice.

The effect in the Persian empire is even more dramatic. As Isaiah prophesies, the Persian rulers take on the role of the "anointed" kings of the Davidic dynasty. They become Yahweh's servants and shepherds, who build Jerusalem, protect the Jews from their enemies, and restore the ruined temple (Isa 44:24—45:7). When Israel returns to the land in a second exodus, there are no plagues, no repeat of Passover, no deadly Red-Sea baptism. There doesn't need to be. Instead of resisting Yahweh's demands, the Persians set Israel free. Cyrus is the Moses of the new Exodus. Israel doesn't need to plunder Persia because the Persians supply them with all the materials they need to rebuild the temple (Ezra 1:5–11).

The church takes over this Jewish mission. Christians are model citizens, seeking the peace of the city. As the church's mission goes forward, high-placed Jews are converted or replaced by believing Jews or converted Gentiles. Over the following centuries, Christian communities become the moral center in Roman city after Roman city, and Christian charity becomes the welfare system of the empire. As the Philippians fear, the customs of the church displace the customs of Romans.

Conclusion

Acts doesn't tell of any converted kings. No Constantine appears, no Charlemagne or Vladimir or Tiridates. Yet the story of Acts presses toward Christendom. Through Spiritual and political battles, through suffering and service, Christians rise to positions of authority as advisors to kings. Eventually, kings will submit to the King of kings and, like Nebuchadnezzar, confess their allegiance to the kingdom of God. The church builds herself as a saving vessel within the Roman world. Eventually, the whole Roman world finds its home in Jesus' ark. Eventually it's official: The heirs of the apostles pilot the Roman ship of state.

5   VESSELS OF SALVATION

> ... *the ark, in which a few, that is, eight persons,*
> *were brought safely through the water.*
> 1 Peter 3:20

After Yahweh forms Adam, He plants an enclosed garden and causes every tree to grow there (Gen 2:7–8). Noah turns trees into gopher wood lumber to build a nautical garden (Gen 6:14). Noah's ark is a sanctuary, measured and divided—like the tabernacle and temple—into three zones. The ark is a new Eden, the first man-made sanctuary on earth.

Every sanctuary is made after the pattern of the heavenly sanctuary (Exod 25:9, 40). As "heaven-on-earth," the sanctuary sets the pattern for the world. The liturgical work of the sanctuary is a model for the political work of kings in the land. Liturgical culture models and renews world culture. The beauty and glory of the sanctuary is to be replicated in the beauty and glory outside. Like the sanctuary, the land is to be a place of food and festivity, joy and communion. During the ideal reign of Solomon, every Israelite lived in joy under his own vine and fig tree (1 Kgs 4:25). Every house and town is remade according to the pattern of the temple. "Thy will be done on earth as it is in heaven" can be translated as "Thy will be done in the land as in the temple, in the world as in the church."

Noah's ark is a microcosm *because* it's a sanctuary. The ark's three decks correspond to the three stories of Yahweh's cosmic house—heaven, earth, and sea. Like the firmament, the ark has a window (Gen 6:16; cf. Mal 3:10). It floats over the formless void of the deep (cf. Gen 1:2), a miniature of land + firmament. Like creation itself, the ark contains all living things. Eight men and women enter the ark, and Noah is a new Adam, herding a pair of every kind of bird, beast, and creeping thing (cf. Gen 1:20, 26), seven of every clean animal, into the ark (Gen 6:19–20; 7:2). Noah stores the ark with plants for food (Gen 6:21), and the ark itself is made from plants.

In fact, the account of the ark follows the order of creation. Yahweh forms a three-story universe (Genesis 1:1–10), and Noah builds a three-story ark (Gen 6:16). Yahweh places Adam and Eve in the garden (Gen 2:8, 21–22) and brings Noah and his family into the ark (Gen 6:18). Yahweh gathers cattle, beasts, and birds to Adam to be named (Gen 2:19–20), and Noah gathers birds, beasts, and creeping things into the ark (Gen 6:19–20). At the climax of Genesis 1, Yahweh offers the world to man as food (Gen 1:29–31). At the climax of His instructions to Noah, He commands Noah to take food into the ark (Gen 6:21).

The remarkable difference, of course, is the *maker*. Yahweh makes the original cosmic house and the original sanctuary. Yahweh designs the ark, but *Noah* makes it. As I've said, Noah is the first human to make rightly. He follows Yahweh's instructions and becomes a Godlike creator, capable of creating a cosmos. His manmade microcosm saves the Creator's macrocosm. After the flood, Noah and his family and all the animals emerge from the ark to start the world over again. Noah preserves seeds of the old world so he can plant them in a new creation.

VESSELS OF SALVATION

His ark is a saving vessel, not for a few scattered souls but for the *world*.

Today, the Carpenter of Nazareth, true man, is still at work building a microcosmic sanctuary, the church. As we've seen, *we* build His body alongside Him. The church is the artwork of the Son and Spirit; it's also the work of master artisans like Paul (1 Cor 3:10) and the millions of Spirit-filled believers who share the work of "edifying" the church. We're *all* Bezalels and Oholiabs (Exod 31:1–11) since we all receive Jesus' Spirit of skill (Acts 2:17; 1 Cor 12:13; cf. Isa 11:1–2). Together, we build ourselves into the ark that is also the body, Bride, and church of Jesus.

Like the ark, the church receives and preserves the treasures of the world (Rev 21:24) so they can be purged, transfigured, and brought out again to adorn creation. As worlds collapse, the world's riches are kept safe in the ark of the church. All things are gathered into the church so that all things can disembark into a new creation. Noah performs this magic only once, but Jesus does it continuously. Treasures flow continuously into the ark of Christendom. The church has received the treasures of Greek and Roman art, philosophy, and politics, to purify them and bring them to fulfillment. It will plunder the gold of China, Japan, and India, of the Masai and Zulu, of Arabia and Iraq and Afghanistan. Treasures from the city of man enter the city of God so they can return to the city of man, renewed. The city of man enters the ark of God so it can become more perfectly what it's supposed to be, more perfectly an image of heavenly Jerusalem.

The church pilots the world. What happens in the holy church guides what happens outside. If the church is unfaithful, leaves her first love, and turns to false teachers, Jesus will remove the lampstand and abandon the house (Rev 2—3). If the church keeps her lamps burning, continuously supplied by the oil of the Spirit, the world will be full of light. Sanctuaries are springs. They can flow with poison (Rev 10–11) or with life-giving waters

(Ezek 47; Rev 22:1–5). The church is the new covenant sanctuary—a spring of life or a source of death.

This is imagery, but not *mere* imagery. It's the way the world works. It describes what the church has always been and done, what she will always be and do. Within the ark of the church, Jesus incubates new forms of social and economic life, new initiatives of work and creativity, new forms of charity, new modes of instruction, new artistic subjects and standards of beauty. The church is the nursery of the kingdom, the ark that preserves, purges, and transforms the treasures of the world. She's the place where the new heavens and earth first take form.

To return to chapter 1: Human beings are created in the image of a Creator. We're made for making. In Adam, we mis-make and mis-speak, but in the Last Adam we are re-made into godly speakers and makers. The church is the forge where our making and speaking is smelted and shaped. As the church's history is scripted by Scripture, as we practice the apostolic customs of *koinonia*, as we battle Spiritual and political enemies, we remake the social worlds around us.

Remaking Makers

Jesus remakes our making by first re-making *us* as makers. He does this in the liturgy, where we are molded into the shape of Jesus. Worship is *leitourgia*, the work of the people. Our postures inscribe humility, attention, and rest on our bodies. In song, we tune our life's breath to the praise of God. In prayer, we cast our cares on the one who cares for us; in common prayer, each of us has voice before the King of all.

All this activity is grounded in a more fundamental passivity. Our giving arises from a more fundamental reception. Liturgy is the work of the people of God, but more fundamentally, it's the work of God *on* the people. It is the Lord's gracious service to us, gifts of God for the people of God. Every week, Jesus puts on the servant's apron to wash the feet of His disciples.

Jesus remakes us by restoring us to priesthood. Man's first vocation is priestly, and his first labor is the labor of the sanctuary (Gen 2:15). All making in the land and world reflects the pattern of priestly serving and guarding. All our making in the world is formed and re-formed by our participation in the priestly work of the sanctuary. As priests, we receive God's gifts with thanks; as priests, we offer our makings to God in praise. Our priestly work is itself a gift of God. By the Spirit, we edify one another and are built up together as the body of Christ. As we carry out the liturgy in step with the Spirit, we are the self-constructing ark that is a microcosm and model for the world.

We often focus on the liturgy's power to renew minds and souls, but Jesus renews bodies too. He's a healer, the divine Physician. He gives sight to the blind and hearing to the deaf, loosens the tongues of the dumb, straightens limbs and cleanses lepers, casts out demons that slash and beat the bodies they possess. Ancient pagans have their Asclepius. But no ancient myth tells of a High God who comes near to mingle and mix with the diseased and demon-possessed. In no mythology or philosophy does the High God show pity for His creatures.

When the apostles receive the Spirit, the apostles continue Jesus' ministry, healing the lame and expelling demons (Acts 3:1–5; 5:12–16; 20:7–12). The church is and has always been a place of healing, and that healing takes form in the quasi-sacrament of anointing (Jas 5:13–18). The sick call for the elders of the church, who anoint with oil and pray over the sick, while the sick confess their sins. Healing is embedded in the liturgical life of the church.

From those seeds—the seeds of a gospel of healing and a rite of anointing—grow the unprecedented Christian attention to health care. Pagans have their medical philosophers like Galen, just as they have their gods of healing. But the Christian mission of healing is qualitatively different. Like Jesus, Christians are "incarnated" among the sick. When plagues and pandemics hit Roman cities, pagans fled, including Galen. Christians stayed to nurse the sick to health. Over time, they developed institutions like the hospital and techniques of healing that were unknown in the ancient world. In the sanctuary-ark of the church, Jesus nourishes new forms of compassion, which, over the centuries, have transformed the world.

Loosening Tongues

We gather in the Lord's presence on the Lord's Day to receive the Word of the Lord at the Lord's table. We are brought into the Triune conversation, united to the Son by the breath of His Spirit. In worship, we hear the Word read, taught, and preached. We sing the Word and pray the Word. We respond to the Word with the Word. Christian worship should be drenched, saturated, flooded with the Word.

When it is, the liturgy produces new forms of speaking and writing outside the sanctuary. To prepare sermons, preachers study biblical texts. They learn biblical languages and refine techniques for historical research and literary interpretation. Nothing like the medieval "fourfold" method of interpretation existed in the pre-Christian world. Over centuries, that method developed into a complex method of reading that preserves history and fact, while discerning also the blossoms of Spiritual meaning that unfold within events. The fourfold is more than a method of reading. It's a biblical theology of history, society, and politics.

As Augustine says, every form of study serves biblical interpretation and teaching. To know what Jesus means when He says, "Be wise as serpents," you need to know something about the cunning habits of serpents. To know what happens to the

Jews between the end of the Old Testament and the beginning of the New, you need to study the books of the Maccabees and Ben Sirach, the visions of Enoch, the historical work of Philo and Josephus. To grasp the long passages of symbolic architecture in Exodus, Kings, and Ezekiel, you need to know something about architecture. You need to know something about political theory to grasp the historical books of the Bible, and those books also serve as a primer of biblical politics.

A full curriculum for Bible readers quickly becomes a curriculum about everything under the sun and many things beyond the sun. Bible teaching incorporates all knowledge outside the Bible. The Bible also serves as a foundry where all knowledge is purged and re-shaped. The liturgy thus inspires a transformation of education. The liberal arts have roots in the classical world, but in the church, they're refreshed by Scripture. The Reformers insisted everyone needed to learn to read so that all could read Scripture. Within the ark of the church, education is oriented to the liturgy. When it emerges from the liturgy, it's something quite different. The apostles' teaching spills out of the ark of the church in new forms of literary culture.

The liturgy is more than teaching. It's formation. It not only fills the heads of worshipers with biblical truth. The Word forms the hearts of worshipers with the beauty and glory of God. The liturgy inscribes honor for God on our bodies. It trains our tongues to speak His Word. It's not merely teaching, but *paideia*, the training of whole persons in the ways of the Lord.

In this way too, the liturgy renews culture. Education is culture, and culture is education. A culture isn't a culture if it lasts only a generation. A way of life must pass as a tradition from generation to generation. *Paedeia*, the Greeks know, is the very essence of culture. By generating new forms of study and education, the Christian church forms a new culture, new habits of speaking and making.

THEOPOLITAN MISSION

Strengthening Hands

Miraculous as it is, the Eucharist isn't a strange anomaly within an impersonal, *in*-significant, mechanistic universe. It discloses the reality deep down things. It shows us that creation is personal and meaningful from top to bottom. Everything we see, touch, taste, and handle is a sign-gift of the Creator's love. In the Eucharist, we receive the world—*this* world, the everyday world of bread and wine, of eating and drinking—as it was meant to be: a joyous communion with the Triune God. The table shows that *every* encounter with reality is an encounter with God.

The Eucharist makes us attentive to creation. Every bird, every blade of grass, every delicate winter rose, every passing cloud, every scurrying squirrel, every flake of sparkling rime is a loving gift from our heavenly Father, to be received with ecstatic thanks. Christians should devote ourselves as closely to the details of our craft or profession as anyone else. Indeed, we have *more* cause to do so since for us there are no dispensable facts, any more than there are dispensable people. *All* the scientist's data, every slab of granite, every drop of paint, every block of wood comes from a Creator who spoke them lovingly into being. If God loves them enough to make them, we must love them too, with all their fascinating intricacies and eccentricities, with all their knotted riddles.

At the table, Jesus remakes our making. The Eucharist is a glimpse of the end of all things. The church gathers at the Lord's table to receive the gifts of God with thanksgiving in the presence of God. All things are moving toward this final destiny, toward translation into the feast of the kingdom. The human race will come to fullness at the marriage supper of the Lamb and His Bride, and all our makings will be transformed by Spirit-guided human labor into adornments of that feast. The table orients our making toward this final destiny. It assures us our labor won't perish but will have a place in an eternal Eucharist.

The table also points to the temporal destinations of our makings. At the Lord's table, we share bread—in some liturgies, bread is passed from hand to hand—an effective emblem of the gift-exchange that makes up the Christian community. We're the one-and-many body because we who are many partake of the one loaf (1 Cor 10:16–17). Bread and wine are paradigms of human products. We do with all our making what we do with the Eucharistic food and drink. We offer everything to God in worship and share all we produce for the edification of the body. Our making isn't simply utilitarian, and yet our makings, even the most needless, are designed to meet needs.

Thanksgiving sanctifies everything (1 Tim 4:4–5). If that's the case, we know the destination of our holy products: Holy things go to holy people. We offer our works to God by distributing them to the people of God as gifts for their edification. Christians are kings who bring our treasures as offerings to adorn the civic most holy place that is the Christian church.

All making involves give-and-take with creation. I take in some bit of the world, work on it, and it becomes part of me. I grow as I take and make; I become more fully who I am created to be. The table I build is *my* table, the book I write, *my* book. At the same time, I give myself to the world, pouring myself into the world to put my stamp on these materials. By making, men and women humanize the world, stamping it with the stamp of the image of God. In that exchange, we commune with the world as labor links the maker, who matures by his making, with the made-thing, which bears the imprint of its creator.

The Eucharist portrays the way making ought to be. At the Lord's table, we commune with the world. Eating becomes the paradigm of our relationship to creation. But the Eucharist also embeds our communion with the world within our communion with God. In holy communion, we commune with God through our makings. The Eucharist renews our relationship with the products of our labor. The minister goes through a series of actions (takes bread, gives thanks, breaks, distributes, eats; takes cup, gives thanks, distributes, drinks) involving things (bread and wine). Through these actions on these things, we encounter a *person*, the Lord Jesus, through His Spirit. That is the reality of all our making and labor. The Eucharist places all our communion with the creation *within* our communion with the Creator.

As God remakes us at the table, He corrects our egotism and our deep belief that our things are *ours*. The Supper infuses all our making with gratitude. We receive the materials and tools of our labor with thanks. We sift, mix, chisel, shape, and reshape the materials with thanks. When we have produced a work, we acknowledge with thanks that, though our work is ours, it is, like bread and wine, a gift from God. When we give thanks, we acknowledge our dependence on the Giver. Like everything we possess, our making is modified by a double possessive. Everything we make is both ours *and* God's.

The Eucharistic liturgy establishes a pattern of Eucharistic living, a life of thanksgiving in all circumstances for everything. All things are consecrated by thanksgiving and prayer (1 Tim 4:4–5). Every human endeavor moves *from* thanks *to* thanks. Even things we make—bread and wine, the work of human hands—are gifts from God. At the table, we're remade to make as priests of a cosmic Eucharist.

We give thanks not only for the materials we receive, but for God's kind providence that guides our making. Beginners believe every discovery is the product of rigorous, thorough, exhaustive engagement, research, experiment, and labor. The historian discovers the decisive, field-changing text because he has spent decades in the dusty archive. The scientist uncovers a secret of the universe because of the comprehensiveness of his controlled experiments. The poet hits upon the right pattern of words after deep reflection. The plumber knows how to design the plumbing because of his deep experience with pipes and couplings.

Any self-aware maker is painfully aware of his limitations and also joyfully aware that insight can come from anywhere. Fresh creativity might come from a chance conversation with a colleague, or a student, or a child, or a grandmother in the early stages of dementia. A researcher spies a forgotten monograph while browsing the stacks or stumbles on an article while surfing the web to check the football scores. A poet overhears a snatch of conversation on the Tube that breaks through his writer's block. A builder figures out how to handle a complicated construction problem while tussling with his toddlers after dinner.

Breakthroughs come at us as unbidden, unbiddable possibilities, and the best makers know how to spin detritus into gold. The Eucharist trains us to take hold of the world *expecting* our Father to provide what we need to complete our work, to polish surfaces of the made-thing we produce. We expect our Father to leave fresh gifts around every corner of the twisting path.

The Eucharist doesn't merely *teach* us we ought to be Eucharistic. Sharing the Eucharist, we are caught up in Eucharist and *become* Eucharist. By the Spirit of the Crucified, we become living sacrifices, offering ourselves and the works of our hands in worship (Rom 12:1–2). This happens only when we commune with Christ and His body in the meal of bread and wine. Once again: Through the table, all our making is folded into His priestly service, which is also our priestly service.

At the table, we're called and called again from idols to communion with the living God. Every time we eat and drink, the Lord issues the double command of the Son of Man: "Worship God," and its corollary, "Flee idols" (1 John 5:21; Rev 22:9). We pulverize idols by bearing witness, and we become witnesses as we *ingest* Jesus, true and faithful *martus* (Rev 3:14). Consuming Him, we're made like Him. By sharing the sacrificial meal, we commit ourselves to self-sacrificing witness. It's more than a commitment: By the Spirit, the feast conforms us to the self-sacrificing witness we consume. It's physically possible to partake of the Lord's table and the table of demons, but it's Spiritually perilous. Having feasted at the marriage supper of the Lamb, we provoke Him to jealousy if we scramble for a seat at the table of demons (1 Cor 10:14–22).

The Lord's table liberates us from the cultural trends, fads, and fashions that grip the mob. Conformed to Christ's death, we rejoice to be outcasts from inner rings. Fashions and fads are often idolatrous at root, and our task is not to worship idols but to expose and expel them. Exposing idols is bound to make us unpopular, as the apostles found. You embarrass an opponent if you call attention to his ignorance or sloppiness. You *enrage* him if you defile the object of his worship. At the least, we'll be ridiculed as we're faithful. But things can get worse. The fashion mob can become a lynch mob. By giving us a share in the cross of Jesus, the Supper prepares us to take up our own cross.

We transform culture by bearing witness, which is always risky. If we're not prepared to suffer professional or vocational death because of our witness to Jesus, if we're not prepared to accept a lower place in the rankings, we have no business putting on the regalia in the first place. If we're not prepared for vocational martyrdom, we despise the table of the Lord, and our makings are nothing worth.

Seeing Eyes, Hearing Ears

Transformed by the Eucharist, our making is freed from pure utility and functionality. Utility is good. A woodworker makes tables for meals, weavers make cloth for clothing, metalworkers make wires for electricity and rebar to strengthen walls. All these forms of making have practical ends. But when we make in order to offer our fruit to God in praise, we transcend mere usefulness. The cobbler doesn't just cover bare feet; he cobbles for the glory of God. At the same time, the sanctuary frees us from the sterile circularity of making for its own sake, the effete snobbery of "art for art's sake." Making Eucharistically, a craftsman makes *for God*. "Art for art's sake" is a sign of decadence. It's a symptom of the decay of liturgy.

Separation of "art" and "life," or "art" and "craft," is a result of the destruction of the liturgy. Many believe art lies in the realm of the imaginary, over-against the mechanical "givenness" of the real world. The liturgy reveals every thing as a gateway to God, every moment a moment to praise. Because liturgy anticipates the justice of the new creation, it's a site of resistance to the violence and injustice of the present age. Only the liturgy holds together ethics and aesthetics, imagination and reality, art and life, beauty and the mundane, affirmation and resistance, already and still to come. Outside the ark of the church, all human making will be drowned in the flood. Cut off from its source in the Eucharist, human making withers. Within the ark of the church, art reaches its destined purpose in praise.

Israel's sanctuaries are the primary sources of Israel's arts. Bezalel and Oholiab are Israel's first named artisans, and they devote their Spirit-given talents to molding gold furniture for the sanctuary, weaving threads to make the tabernacle curtains and the priest's garments, shaping wood for the frame of the tent (Exod 31:1–11). Solomon shows his wisdom by constructing the temple. Skilled or "wise" craftsmen sculpt stone into blocks for the temple, cast a giant bronze sea and tall bronze pillars, carve oil-wood cherubim, and decorate the cedar walls with blossoms and gourds. Israel's music is liturgical music, sung and played by the Levitical choir and orchestra David establishes (1 Chr 25:1–31).

No doubt, there were furniture makers, weavers and tailors,

stonemasons and metalworkers in the villages and towns of Israel. No doubt there were butchers other than the sacred butchers at the altar. But the Bible focuses our attention on sacred craftsmen because the sanctuary is the spring and source of artistic life, of the life of making, which *is* human life.

That biblical pattern is repeated in the history of Christendom. Ancient tragedy ceased to be performed in the early Christian era. Drama was reborn in the liturgy, in mystery and miracle plays that enacted biblical stories or taught moralistic lessons to the illiterate multitudes. Western music began in the chants and harmonies of Christian worship.

For a millennium and more, the great architectural styles of the West were church styles—Romanesque, Gothic, neoclassical. Aspects of these styles have classical roots, but they were transformed, sometimes explicitly for theological reasons. Abbot Suger "invented" the Gothic style, with its majestic arches and its stunning glasswork, because he believed light is a material manifestation of the Spirit. Eastern churches and cathedrals were designed to leave people wondering whether they're in heaven or on earth. From the church, new styles and techniques flowed out to change the way we build Parliament houses and palaces.

In Scripture and Christian history, visual arts, architecture, and music come to birth as *liturgical* arts. Human making is purged and renewed in the sanctuary as the sanctuary, patterned by heaven, becomes the pattern for the world. Arts and artistic skills are born or reborn within the bosom of mother church.

Godly Rule

The church produces new forms of political life, especially in the relations between church and state, religion and power. Like literary culture, like bread-making and wine-making, like architecture, art, and music, political power is transformed from the sanctuary. It begins with the restoration of Adam's priestly vocation. Earthly rule resembles heavenly rule when it passes through the liturgy.

We can see this in the history of Israel's regime of "church and state." Prior to Sinai, Israel has no sanctuary, no priestly class, and a much simpler and less explicit sacrificial and purity system. Once Israel arrives at the mountain, though, Aaron and his sons are ordained as priests (Exod 19; Lev 8—9), with exclusive access to the altar and the tabernacle (cf. Exod 29:37). Priests participate in every sacrificial rite at the tabernacle: the daily ascension offerings, the offerings brought by individual Israelite worshipers, and the massive sacrifices on feast days.

No lay Israelites, including elders, are permitted to perform these rites. In fact, every lay Israelite is excluded from the tent; the "stranger" who attempts to enter is executed (Num 1:51; 3:10, 38). Once Yahweh consecrates the tabernacle with His glory, not even Moses is allowed to enter (Exod 40:34–38). The "church" of the sanctuary is governed and run by priests, not by civil rulers.

On the other hand, priests have responsibilities for maintaining the holiness and purity of the land. Difficult criminal cases are brought to a priest (Deut 17:8–13), who inquires of Yahweh, perhaps using the Urim and Thummim. Whatever the priest decides is carried out: "According to the mouth of the law which they teach you, and according to the verdict which they tell you, you shall do" (Deut 17:11). Whoever refuses a priest's verdict is put to death (Deut 17:12). Before Israel goes to war, the (high?) priest warns them not to fear or panic because Yahweh gives victory (Deut 20:2–4), and priests lead the army at Jericho (Josh 6). Moses generalizes, "Every dispute and every stroke shall be according to [the priests'] mouth" (Deut 21:5).

Under the monarchy, power is centralized in the capital, first Hebron and then Jerusalem. David has a small court, consisting of military leaders, a bodyguard, secretaries, and priests

(2 Sam 8:15–18; 20:23–26), as well as overseers of his lands and storehouses (1 Chr 27:25–31). Hushai, Ahitophel, and others serve as counselors to the king (1 Chr 27:32–34). To these, Solomon adds tribal administrators over the "forced labor" that builds the temple and Solomon's palace complex (1 Kgs 4:6; 11:28; 12:1–4). He organizes the land into twelve districts, each led by a deputy who gathers produce to supply the palace one month a year (1 Kgs 4:7–19). The abundance and elegant choreography of Solomon's court is enough to take the breath away from a monarch like Queen Sheba (1 Kgs 10:4–5).

David reorganizes the priests, and Solomon builds the temple, yet the priests retain their monopoly of the sanctuary. When King Uzziah attempts to offer incense at the golden altar inside the temple, Ahaziah the high priest warns him to leave: "It is not for you, Uzziah, to burn incense to Yahweh, but for the priests, the sons of Aaron who are consecrated to burn incense" (2 Chr 26:18). As Uzziah rages at the priests, the Lord strikes his forehead with leprosy, and he remains in isolation for the remainder of his life (2 Chr 26:20–21). Israel's kings aren't gods or priests. They don't run everything. The sanctuary is outside their jurisdiction. The very existence of a separate priesthood limits the scope of royal power. The church blocks the expansion of the state.

Kings can't do priestly things, but priests have significant political authority in the Davidic kingdom. Deuteronomy 17 anticipates a future monarchy, but it's a monarchy under priestly oversight. The king writes out his own copy of Torah in the presence of the priests and is required to study it throughout his life (Deut 17:18–20). Priests are the teachers of Israel (Mal 2:7), including teachers of elders and kings. It's not surprising that priests are included in listings of royal officials (e.g., 2 Sam 8:15–18).

Prophets begin to appear during the monarchy, and they have a prominent role in the governance of the land. Samuel anoints Saul and David, confronts Saul for his various sins, and guides David as he makes his way to the throne. Nathan, David's court prophet, condemns him for seizing Bath-sheba and killing her husband, Uriah (2 Sam 12:1–15). Ahab has his own court prophets, who advise him about his planned military excursion to Ramoth-gilead (1 Kgs 22:1–6).

Though Elijah and Elisha are at odds with Ahab and his descendants, they engage frequently and directly with wicked kings. Elijah organizes a power contest with Ahab's prophets at Mount Carmel (1 Kgs 18:16–46) and confronts him about his murder of Naboth (1 Kgs 21:17–29). Despite antagonism with the dynasty of Ahab, Elisha is in the entourage of Jehoram as the king goes to suppress a Moabite rebellion (2 Kgs 3:4–20). Elisha gives a favorable prophecy about the deliverance of Samaria from an Aramean siege (2 Kgs 7:1), and his servant Gehazi has access to the king's court (2 Kgs 8:1–6).

In Samuel and Kings, prophets confront kings mainly for their personal sins and failings. Samuel rebukes Saul for not waiting to sacrifice and for failing to carry out the ban against the Amalekites (1 Sam 13, 15), and Nathan confronts David about adultery and murder (2 Sam 12:1–15). The writing prophets engage in prophetic punditry, judging kings, lesser rulers, and the entire nation for "policy" failures and their rebellion against the Lord's justice. Isaiah condemns Judah's rulers for failure to protect orphans and widows from exploitation (Isa 1:16–17) and for bribery (Isa 1:21–23), and he delivers "Woes" against those who gobble up land (Isa 5:8–10), who confuse standards of good and evil (Isa 5:20), and who enact evil statutes (Isa 10:1–4).

Jeremiah counsels King Zedekiah to submit to Nebuchadnezzar and warns that the nation will face sword, famine, and pestilence if he resists (Jer 27:1–15). Ezekiel prophesies against the "shepherds of Israel" (Ezek 34:2), a royal rather than a priestly metaphor. Israel's shepherds fatten themselves on the flock, fail to care for the sick, diseased, and broken; the flock of Israel is scattered for lack of shepherding (Ezek 34:3–6). Amos rebukes Israel for rejecting the laws of Yahweh and for abuse of the poor, sexual promiscuity, and cruel treatment of wage laborers (Amos 2:4–8), and Micah condemns prophets, seers, and priests as well as the cannibal kings who rip their subjects in pieces and cook their flesh (Mic 3:1–12). The sanctuary and priests set institutional limits to the state. Prophets remind kings they're responsible to God and subject to His judgment. Priests and prophets lay out the pattern of godly rule and call rulers to conform to it.

During the exile, Israel has no temple or king. Jewish communities are independent of the Gentile state. Though embedded in the empire, they form separate communities. Yet Israel continues to carry out her priestly and prophetic vocation, including her political role. When emperors command faithful Jews to worship idols, the Jews defy them (Dan 2, 6). Yet Jews advise Gentile rulers, both to protect the Jewish people and to pursue justice. Thick boundaries protect the Israelite church, but the church speaks Yahweh's Word even to non-Jewish states.

The church emerges from Judaism, both in Judea and in the diaspora. Like the exilic Jewish communities, the church is a self-governing community with its own customs of worship, teaching, and prayer. The church relates to the Roman empire as exilic Jewish communities did. Jeremiah instructs the exiles to seek the peace of Babylon, and the apostles regularly issue similar instructions to the early Christians. Echoing Jeremiah, Paul tells the Romans to submit to the powers, which are established for their good (Rom 13:1–7). Paul urges prayer for kings and authorities so Christians can lead quiet and peaceable lives (1 Tim 2:1–2). Peter echoes Paul: "Submit yourselves for the Lord's sake to every human institution," to kings and governors. By doing right, Christians will "silence the ignorance of foolish men" (1 Pet 2:13–17).

But the new covenant also gives birth to a new political reality. The primary innovation is the character of the church.

In a sense, the church makes exile permanent. The church will never be settled in *a* land with *a* temple and *a* king. She will always be scattered among many states and societies that are more or less responsive to the gospel. By welcoming Gentiles on equal terms with Jews, the church becomes a cosmopolitan communion, a geographically catholic church without any necessary links to any land, race, or political order.

Churches are outposts of a heavenly kingdom, akin to foreign embassies among the nations, governed always by the high King, Jesus. As such, the church is outside the jurisdiction of kings, governors, presidents, and prime ministers. As in Israel, the existence of the church sets institutional limits to the scope of the state. States can break down the barrier and take over the church. But if the church is faithful, there will be opposition. Any ruler who tries to intrude on the sanctuary should remember Uzziah. He should remember Jesus, who reigns from Zion with a rod of iron.

The church is independent of the state, yet the church takes over Israel's priestly-prophetic role of teaching and correcting rulers. Pastors and bishops call kings to submit to the Lord Jesus, for they are His servants, and they submit by listening to the voice of Jesus in the church and by honoring His Bride.

Meanwhile, the church nurtures virtuous leaders, who care for their people with pastoral love and concern. The church disciplines leaders and lays out standards of godly rule. Within the church, a new kind of prince comes into being—a saintly prince, whose public life is full of the fruits of the Spirit, who rules with love, joy, peace, patience, gentleness, and self-control (Gal 5:22). When kings enter the ark of Christendom, they're taught to govern with justice, to seek peace. They become rain on the mown grass, enabling their peoples to flourish (Psa 72).

Conclusion

The church is a self-constructing ark, built around pulpit and table, song and communion. Each of these liturgical forms generates fresh political and cultural realities. The pulpit begets literary culture, renewing language and education. The Eucharist transforms human labor, transfiguring and sanctifying all human making. Rites of anointing blossom in charitable health care, while liturgical art, music, and architecture generate new forms of artistic expression in the city of man. By protecting her independence from the state, the church is the impetus for a new political order of justice, accountability, and freedom. By teaching the Word to kings, the church fosters godly rule.

To transform the city of man, the church only needs to do what she does, to be what she is. She needs only to teach, preach, sing, pray, break bread. Within the ark of Christendom, she need only keep the customs of the apostles, and all will be changed.

EPILOGUE

Theopolitan Mission is written in generalities. I've been writing about permanent demands and patterns of Christian mission, demands and patterns that hold in all times and places. Always and everywhere, the church is the ark of the Greater Noah, building itself as a microcosm that preserves and renews the cosmos. Always and everywhere, the church is the presence of Jesus by the Spirit—baptizing, teaching, breaking bread, continuing in prayer. Always and everywhere, the lives of Christians are conformed to the suffering and glory of the Christ.

But the patterns I've described apply with particular force to the first readers of this book, in Anno Domini 2021. A flood is coming, and while the storm clouds gather, we need to get busy building the ark of Jesus.

Noah builds his ark because Yahweh tells him, "Behold, I, even I, am bringing the flood of water upon the earth to destroy all flesh in which is the breath of life, from under heaven; everything that is on earth shall perish. But I will establish my covenant with you" (Gen 6:17–18). Noah's world is about to be swept away. He preserves the world by gathering a little world into the ark and riding out the storm until Yahweh opens the door on a new creation.

Jesus is the Greater Noah because He enters the world at a similar moment in history. As John the Baptist warns, the axe is already at the root, and the Lord is kindling a fire to burn fruitless trees (Matt 3:7–10). Jesus urges repentance for the same reason: The arrival of the kingdom is the arrival of judgment. That judgment will fall before His disciples die. It will be like the days of Noah (Matt 24:37–38; Luke 17:26–27). All the apostles say the same thing: The Lord is at hand. It is the last hour. Jesus is coming quickly.

Remember the historical context. From the exile to Jesus, Israel is nestled within a succession of ancient empires. In the time of Jesus and His apostles, the world is bipolar, its foci in Jerusalem and Rome, the capital of Jews and the capital of Gentiles. *That* world is about to be washed away. Before the generation of the apostles ends, Jerusalem will be in ruins, the temple will be demolished, and the Roman world will be shaken to its foundations. The sun will go dark, the moon will turn bloody, and stars will fall. The clock is running out. The universe of Jerusalem-and-Rome is about to fall, and great will be its fall (Matt 24:29–31, 34).

As Jesus' ark, the church fills the same role as Noah's ark. As the world is shattered, the apostles call and baptize men and women and children into the body of Christ. There they attend to the apostles' teaching, break bread together, practice *koinonia*, devote themselves to continual prayer, thanksgiving, and praise. In the liturgy and the liturgy of Christian life, they form seedpods of new creation. Once the clouds clear, the seeds germinate and grow.

It takes a few centuries to see the full fruition of these events. When the Roman empire finally collapses for good, a new civilization is born from the womb of Christ's Bride. Monks preserve Greek and Roman learning and found monasteries as

EPILOGUE

centers of prayer and worship and sources of technical innovation. Bishops care for the poor and sick in the cities, build churches and cathedrals, commission painters and sculptors and composers. Christendom produces new forms of political organization, guaranteeing many of the basic liberties we still enjoy in modern republics and democracies. Individual rights, personal liberty, constitutional government, the rule of law, limits to state power, the equal dignity of all: All of these are gifts of the church as it purged and transformed the political inheritance of Greece and Rome. They're gifts of Christ's reign.

Since the sixteenth and seventeenth centuries, Western civilization, the heir of Christendom, has become the foundation of global civilization. Even the values and politics of the secular Enlightenment and contemporary radicalism depend on treasures inherited from Christianity. For hundreds of years, the civilization that emerged from the ark of the church has molded the entire world.

At the beginning of the twenty-first century, we're entering a new epoch of world history. Non-Western nations and continents are on the rise. China dominates east Asia and is extending its economic power into the Middle East up to the edge of Europe and deep into Africa. India has become a global player. By the middle of this century, Africa will have over 2 billion people, and by 2100, one of every three human beings will be African. Africa is coming of age economically and will be the center of Christianity during this century. All of these up-and-coming regions depend on Western civilization's achievements and thus are the late fruit of Christendom. Yet, politically, economically, and religiously, the Western world is losing the dominant place it has occupied for half a millennium.

Meanwhile, Western civilization is disintegrating from within. Western intellectuals have lost confidence in our own civilization. Enlightenment values are under attack and in retreat.

Western civilization has been severed from its Christian roots as churches decline in both numbers and influence. Ancient Israel is judged when they worship idols, commit sexual perversions, and murder the innocent. Western nations are guilty of all of these. We murder millions of unborn babies a year, and our militaries shed innocent blood in the far corners of the world. We now honor abominations like sodomy and turn a blind eye when surgeons reassemble girls into boys and boys into girls. The West has turned from Jesus to the false gods of Science, Reason, Power, Progress, Mammon, or to the equally false gods of Equality and Choice.

A flood is coming. It's already sweeping away the world as we know it. The world we know will be submerged as the Lord turns the world upside down and gives it a sharp shake (Hag 2:6–7).

It's *not* the end of everything. Creation will survive, and civilization will be reborn. Jesus will steer the ark of His church through the storm. As the clouds gather, as the thunder begins to roll, as the deluge crashes down, we're called to continue the often-imperceptible work of building the ark of Jesus. With our lives scripted by the Scriptures that reveal the Christ, we cling to the apostolic gospel, gather to break bread, share our material and Spiritual gifts, offer a continuous sacrifice of prayer and song. We preach the good news in false churches and public squares, endure the rage of the mob, suffer with Jesus so we may share His glory. We confront idols and demons and call all men from darkness to light, from Satan to the living God (Acts 26:18). In the Last Adam, we're made right-makers, grateful makers whose making is an act of worship. Some will slip, lizard-like, into palaces (Prov 30:28) and gain a hearing before Prime Ministers and Presidents.

As we do these things, we preserve the treasures of the past and, by the alchemy of the Spirit, transfigure ancient treasures into new. When the storm is over and the flood waters recede, we'll have and be the seeds of a new creation. We'll flow like living

EPILOGUE

water to fertilize the wasteland.

If you're a Christian, *that's* what you're doing. Your life may not look like a big deal. You're kind to your neighbors, serve your brothers and sisters in church, gather each week to receive God's Word and God's Bread. You train and teach your children as disciples; you love your husband or wife. You're an honest and productive employee, an attentive employer, an entrepreneur or bureaucrat in a well-established institution. You do and make, but no one notices.

Maybe you're a pastor or leader in a church. You preach and teach, lead worship, and preside at the Lord's table. You visit the hospital and the homebound seniors of the congregation, plan and execute evangelistic and service programs, baptize and catechize the children of the church. You're a big fish, but your pond is small and sometimes looks more like a puddle.

You feel invisible, but that's an optical illusion. You're participating in the biggest project imaginable. You're joining with millions of others to build the self-building ark of Jesus. Through your witness and labor, a new world is taking form. You're fighting the battle of the ages. You're constructing the city of God among the cities of men in order to transform the cities of men to become more like the city of God. *Nothing* is small in the kingdom of Jesus.

There's nothing to fear. We live in joy and expectant hope. Jesus is in the boat, and He calms the seas. The Carpenter of Nazareth will pilot His ark until it rests on a new Ararat, a new Eden, the garden-city where the river of life flows.

FOR FURTHER READING

Jenkins, Philip. *The Next Christendom*. Third Edition. Oxford: Oxford University Press, 2011.

Jenson, Robert. "Eschatology" in William T. Cavanaugh and Peter Manley Scott, eds., *The Wiley Blackwell Companion to Political Theology*. Second edition. Hoboken, NJ: John Wiley & Sons, 2019.

Jordan, James B. *The Sociology of the Church*. Eugene, OR: Wipf & Stock, 1999.

Jordan, James B. *Christendom and the Nations*. Monroe, LA: Athanasius Press, 2019.

Leithart, Peter J. *Against Christianity*. Moscow, ID: Canon Press, 2003.

Leithart, Peter J. *Deep Comedy*. Moscow, ID: Canon Press, 2006.

Leithart, Peter J. *The Baptized Body*. Moscow, ID: Canon Press, 2007.

Leithart, Peter J. *Solomon Among the Postmoderns*. Grand Rapids: Brazos, 2008.

Leithart, Peter J. *Defending Constantine*. Downers Grove, IL: IVP, 2010.

Leithart, Peter J. *Between Babel and Beast*. Eugene, OR: Cascade, 2012.

Leithart, Peter J. *The End of Protestantism*. Grand Rapids: Baker, 2016.

Leithart, Peter J. *Delivered from the Elements of the World*. Downers Grove, IL: IVP, 2016.

Leithart, Peter J. *The Theopolitan Vision*. Monroe, LA: Athanasius, 2019.

Leithart, Peter J. *Theopolitan Liturgy*. Monroe, LA: Athanasius, 2019.

Leithart, Peter J. *The Ten Commandments*. Bellingham, WA: Lexham Press, 2020.

Leithart, Peter J. *Theopolitan Reading*. Monroe, LA: Athanasius, 2020.

Middleton, J. Richard. "Creation Founded in Love: Breaking Rhetorical Expectations in Genesis 1:1-2:3," in Leonard Jay Greenspoon and Bryan F. LeBeau, eds., *Sacred Text, Secular Times*. Omaha, NE: Creighton University Press, 2000.

www.ingramcontent.com/pod-product-compliance
Lightning Source LLC
Chambersburg PA
CBHW031124080526
44587CB00011B/1098